MW01092514

THE DIGITAL NOMAD SURVIVAL GUIDE

PETER KNUDSON

KATHERINE CONAWAY

Cover

LAUREN HOM

Editor

KATHERINE ROBINSON

CONTENTS

The Digital Nomad Survival Guide
© 2017 Peter Knudson and Katherine Conaway

Cover design © 2017 by Lauren Hom
http://homsweethom.com/

Visit **DigitalNomadHelp.com** for more information.

Special thanks to:

Our illustrator, Lauren, for creating a beautiful cover and fun icons for our survival guide.

Our editor, Katherine #2, for reviewing our drafts in detail and providing helpful outside feedback.

Our family and friends for supporting us and helping spread the word about our project.

Our clients and collaborators for working with us wherever in the world we go.

Our RY2 Battuta family for being an amazing, crazy, and supportive digital nomad community, and Remote Year, for bringing us together in the first place.

BECOMING A DIGITAL NOMAD

WHO SAYS you have to go to an office every day to manage a successful career? That having a home of your own and a routine are the only ways to be a real adult? That the place you're happiest is the place where you were born or where you found your job? That you'll be able to retire one day and *then* travel the world?

We've grown up seeing various models of what it means to be an adult, but the common theme follows the same pattern: get a job, make a home, start a family. That conventional lifestyle is rooted in cultural traditions and historical needs and opportunities.

But it's no longer the only way.

People of all walks of life, all industries and nationalities become digital nomads. Despite wildly different backgrounds, the motivation is consistent: to have a lifestyle that exhibits freedom of choice and is enabled by modern technology and travel.

While many companies are still brick-and-mortar, we are seeing more and more opportunities for remote work. Today, we can choose between hostels, hotels, personal apartments, and co-living spaces. We can bounce from place to place or settle in and stay awhile, go local, seek out adventure, or relish in seclusion.

It's never been easier to get recommendations and make reservations for living arrangements, and plans can be solidified months in advance or hours before arrival. The technology has never been more available or more flexible for creating itineraries and will only continue to improve.

However, with all the options available for people living this lifestyle, it's hard to know **where to start and what will work best for you.**

In *The Digital Nomad Survival Guide*, we share our experiences and insights, plus those of dozens of other digital nomads, to help you join our ranks.

The questions we have to answer paint pictures of your possible future lifestyle and how exciting it is to:

- Select a new place on earth to visit and live (city or nature? hot or cold? busy or chill? familiar or foreign?)
- Scope out a home (apartment, hotel, dorm, or resort? central or isolated?)
- Find a place to work (cafe or coworking? beachfront hammock or desk in an office?)
- Meet new people (through coworking spaces, events, networking, happy hours, pub crawls, yoga, and ways you'd never imagine)
- Explore your new surroundings and seek out adventure (mountains, waterfalls, beaches, landmarks, museums, and more)

Even though we've been on the road for years, making that list and thinking about all the options gets us excited too! That's why we keep living this lifestyle – it's intoxicating and addicting to explore the endless opportunities of working and living around the world.

But this book isn't about *why* you should be a digital nomad. Countless blogs and books already inspire people with stories and images and advice about this lifestyle.

So let's talk about why you *are* here and what we have to offer.

Why You're Here

You – for one reason or another – have decided that you want to live a location-independent lifestyle.

Perhaps you've grown restless staying in one place, or you have decided that you want to travel while still maintaining and growing a career. Or maybe you are already an entrepreneur or freelancer and simply want a change of scenery.

Whatever the reason – you've taken the first step. High five! We know it's a big and exciting decision. Now it's time to turn that decision into your reality, and we're here to help.

Who do you want to be, where, and when?

This is the central opportunity of the digital nomad lifestyle: trying out a new life for a finite period of time anywhere on earth, and then doing it again (and again and again). The challenge (though it can be a fun one) is planning it.

You are about to begin your adventure – leaving your comfortable routine and entering a world where you might not know where you will be next week or next month, who you will travel with, or where you will call home. (Feel free to revisit Dr. Seuss's *Oh The Places You'll Go* at any time.)

We encourage you to embrace that kind of unknown and variety – it will be motivation to wake up in the morning and produce your best work to make your new life work.

Why We're Here

This is the book we wish we had read a few years ago. We had jobs, we had dreams, and we had travel experience - but we didn't really know how to go from "normal life" to being a digital nomad.

Now that we have the experience of making that transition and living this lifestyle for years, we want to share clear advice and recommendations for others looking to make the change.

For everyone, overcoming the inertia of routine is difficult and, frankly, often scary. Then there are all the details that have to be planned in advance (…or do they?).

What do I pack? Where should I go? How much money do I need? What phone and plan should I use? What happens if I lose a credit card?

After years on the road (you can learn more about us, Peter and Katherine, in the *About Us* section at the end), we have a much clearer understanding of what works and what doesn't, what's good and what's bad, what we liked and what we wished we avoided. Those insights have been very helpful for us as we continue to plan our lives as digital nomads.

Every day, we hear from people asking about what we do and how. We regularly check Facebook groups and online forums to see the same questions repeated by people around the world.

So we decided to pool our knowledge and write *The Digital Nomad Survival Guide* - a reference manual about how to get started and survive being a digital nomad.

We looked in popular forums for common questions and pain points, went back through our own records (financial, travel, work, and personal), talked to friends we've met on the road, referenced blog posts that are helpful and informative, surveyed digital nomads, and researched favorite tools and apps.

Being a digital nomad means you'll be moving frequently while maintaining your career in different environments. This book will provide you with useful and specific knowledge about travel, housing, work, and socializing to help you manage your new lifestyle over the long run.

We advise reading the book first all the way through as it's an interconnected system with several threads running through multiple chapters. We've worked to create focus chapters around specific topics and have organized them in order of how we expect a new digital nomad would need to work through them for initial planning.

However, you can hop around as fits your needs and revisit chapters throughout your time as a digital nomad.

Our chapters include narratives and anecdotes, specific references and suggestions for tools + apps + places, Pro Tips, examples of budgets and packing lists, checklists, and more. We advise developing a system for taking notes and tracking your research, as this will be the foundation of your own personal survival guide.

Following the end of the last chapter, you'll find several bonus sections – interviews with digital nomads, a *Digital Nomad Tool Kit* (where we've compiled the self-assessment, budget, packing list, and all our recommendation + resource links together), and data from our digital nomad census. There's also an *About Us* section with information about our background, work, and travel experience.

If we can make this transition easier for one more person – to help them realize that yes, they can manage the elusive lifestyle of traveling while working – then all the hard work that went into this book will have been worth it.

Of course, this is not a substitute for any professional advice, whether financial, legal, health related, or otherwise. Please consult licensed professionals as needed and exercise common sense (always! and when applying our advice to your life).

Benefits and Challenges of the Lifestyle

For most people coming from a stable lifestyle, even if they want to make the change, the loss of control and the adjustment to a different standard of living on a regular basis can be a huge challenge.

Instead of having a home, a job in an office, and a routine, knowing where you go, what you do, and when you do it – now *everything* is up to you (or forces well beyond your control), and your daily life is often completely flexible.

That freedom is, after all, the point of becoming a digital nomad. But it is also one of the burdens that can lead to burnout - routine helps us simplify our lives and focus our attention where it's most needed.

Becoming a digital nomad will help you gain insights into your strengths and weaknesses, and the transition may help you discover what you really need to be successful and happy and healthy - but it will be a process with considerable trial and error and many hard days.

It's not always as beautiful as the Instagram pictures will have you believe. It can get messy, lonely, and frustrating. Plus, sand gets *everywhere*.

Whether it's adjusting to time zones, local foods, cultural differences, working conditions, homesickness, loneliness, stress, finances, or any other number of challenges, there will be many moments that are physically and emotionally exhausting.

We encourage you to constantly assess your priorities, keep your "why" in mind, and remember to be patient and practice self-care. (Don't worry, we talk about all of this in various chapters.)

Being a digital nomad is *not* a long-term vacation – it's a lifestyle. The focus of your experience should be on making sure it's one that works for you over the long run.

We are here to help you prepare yourself well, navigate some of the most common pitfalls, and work toward making this lifestyle a healthy and sustainable one.

A Caveat

This is inevitably very much a book of the moment - so it may become dated sooner than we'd like. The factors and information we discuss are always and quickly changing: technology evolves constantly, foreign policy and international relations impact safety and travel to different cities and countries, the economy impacts buying power and demand for work.

So while our advice here is rooted in our experience and research, it's based on the reality of 2016. At publication, it's February 2017, and many things are in a state of flux.

The rest of this year and the ones that follow are sure to yield circumstances that create both opportunities and challenges, shift world politics, offer improved technology, and change best practices for being a digital nomad.

But that doesn't mean the information and advice we provide here will expire and become irrelevant - much of what we share is big-picture strategy as well as specific recommendations.

Strategy is the core of determining your own approach to your new lifestyle, and you'll **use our suggestions as a starting point to find the best technology, resources, and information for your personal needs**.

Good luck!

PETER + KATHERINE

You can keep up with any relevant updates and find more information on our website: DigitalNomadHelp.com.

SELF-ASSESSMENT

WE'VE CREATED this *Self-Assessment* to help you consciously prepare as the first step in becoming a digital nomad. Our chapters will refer back to this assessment as a resource to help you determine which of our suggestions and advice best fit you and your future lifestyle as a digital nomad. (You can also find it in the *Digital Nomad Tool Kit* at the end.)

The clarity you'll gain around your reasons and needs will help you stay focused on your priorities during your planning phase as well as once you are living this lifestyle.

Because you'll be constantly moving and changing your environment, you'll need to consider these elements frequently, and perhaps adjust them as time goes on. Adapting and evolving and changing your mind are not only allowed, they're encouraged! Why travel the world and experience new things if you don't let anything change the way you think and operate?

Let's get started!

Our advice on how to approach this self-assessment:

1. Read the questions first.
2. Start a note (on paper or your computer), and answer without editing yourself—think stream-of-consciousness responses.
3. Review your answers and note patterns and inconsistencies.
4. Create a document on your computer and write down your responses, editing if needed to get clear and definitive answers or hierarchies.

We will address many of these questions throughout the book. This initial assessment is primarily meant to get your planning started and creative juices flowing.

Digital Nomad

1. How did you first hear about the digital nomad lifestyle?
2. What appeals to you? Why are you excited about it?
3. What aspects do you think will be difficult for you?
4. What does it mean to be a digital nomad (to you)?
5. What does it mean to do it successfully?
6. Who do you know that is already a digital nomad? Whose lifestyle is an example for you?
7. Why do you want to be a digital nomad? [aim for a direct, specific, and simple statement]

Circumstances

1. Where do you currently live? [location and residence type]
2. Who are the important people in your life? [family, partner, friends, employer, clients, coworkers, etc]
3. How will you becoming a digital nomad impact them?
4. Do you have pets, a home, a car, and other major considerations that need to be resolved before you can leave?

Work

1. What is your current job and employment status?
2. Is it already remote or is it possible to do it remotely?
3. Have you discussed it with your employer / clients yet?

4. What technology do you need for work? [hardware and software]
5. How many hours a week do you need to work?
6. Do you need to work in a specific time zone?
7. What work challenges do you anticipate as part of becoming a digital nomad / working remotely?
8. What opportunities will become available as a digital nomad / working remotely? [professionally and personally]
9. What are your favorite parts of your job / work? What are you best at doing?

Travel

1. How long are you planning to be a digital nomad? [up to 6 months, 1-2 years, 2+ years, etc]
2. Why that time frame?
3. Do you have anywhere you need to be on certain dates?
4. How many places do you want to go / how frequently do you want to move?
5. Where are you most excited to visit and live? Why?
6. Will you be traveling alone, with someone else, or joining a group?
7. What country's citizenship / passport will you use for your travels?

Money

1. What do you currently spend on housing each month? Each day? [divide monthly by 30]
2. What do you currently spend on food each month? Each day?

3. What do you currently spend on social + entertainment each month? Each day? [movies, shows, games, happy hours, nights out, etc]
4. What will your estimated monthly income be as a digital nomad?
5. How much will you want to spend on activities each month? [side trips, adventures, classes, big dollar experiences, etc]

Possessions

1. What are a few of your favorite things?
2. What clothes and belongings do you absolutely need?
3. Do you have any medical prescriptions, devices, or other belongings that you need to travel with?
4. What material items in your current life can you live without?
5. What do you want to do with the clothes, furniture, and belongings that you won't bring with you?

Personal

1. What are your daily routines?
2. What do you need in your home environment to be comfortable and relaxed?
3. What do you need in your work environment to be successful and productive?
4. What do you need in your personal life and relationships to feel supported and happy?
5. Do you need significant time alone or do you prefer to be with others?

Congratulations on taking the first concrete step!

THE DIGITAL NOMAD SURVIVAL GUIDE

FINANCES

"How much do I need to make in order to do be a digital nomad?"

THIS QUESTION IS one of the most frequently asked by new digital nomads, which is why we're tackling it in the first chapter. The answer, however, like many in this book, will depend more on you, your needs, and your wants than anything we can tell you. But we can help you define your answer.

In this chapter, you will learn how to budget as a digital nomad, the best financial tools to help you stay afloat, and the best practices that keep long-term digital nomads in the black year after year.

Real Talk: Money

Many people are afraid to talk about money, much less be truly aware of their spending habits. But a healthy financial situation (and an honest awareness of it) is critical to any sustainable lifestyle, whether you're living at home or on the road.

If your finances aren't in order, you'll struggle to start a nomadic lifestyle and will likely soon find yourself faced with deciding whether to return home or make the necessary changes that allow you to continue traveling and working remotely.

Before you dive into your digital nomad lifestyle, spend time reviewing your accounts, monitoring your spending, and deciding upon a realistic and responsible budget.

Many people think just because a country (say, Thailand) has a lower cost of living, then they can get by with little-to-no income. The truth is that there are a lot of factors to consider, and you need to make sure you have a plan before entering a foreign country.

The lifestyle of a digital nomad means you work while you're on the road – otherwise, you're simply taking a holiday. It's important to strike a realistic balance between work and play to appreciate the freedom we originally sought. It's key to structure your finances and budget correctly.

At first, your costs may be on the higher side if this is your first time traveling or living abroad. You won't have the experience to know how to find the best deals in your local area or where the best value accommodations likely are. That's okay! It's a learning process.

You may aim to decrease your costs every month or year that you are a digital nomad, as things become easier and more streamlined. It would be a good idea to reach out to local Facebook or MeetUp groups to get a seasoned digital nomad's take on the best and most affordable places to eat, areas to stay, and ways to save money and not get caught in the "tourist pricing" that seem to be rampant in some cities. (We'll talk more about researching where to go in the *Location Scouting* chapter.)

Or you may plan on a lifestyle that alternates between higher cost-of-living locations and spending more on special experiences with months in less expensive places and living on a tight budget.

Either way, if you know how much your annual budget is, you can plan for high and low months that average out to the correct bottom line over time.

It's up to you how your lifestyle looks and changes, and your budget will either adapt to, or direct, those lifestyle shifts.

Budgeting: Making it All Work

Let's go back to the frequently asked question posed at start of the chapter: *"How much do I need to make in order to do be a digital nomad?"*

We can't presume to answer the question for every city in every country or for every person's specific situation, needs, and preferences. However, we can give you some general guidelines and resources.

In the introduction's self-assessment, we asked several questions to help you determine your current spending habits (monthly and daily) on housing, food, social, and activities.

Do you anticipate wanting to spend a similar amount while traveling, or do you want to increase or decrease your budget? Do you know whether your income will be changing significantly?

Contrary to popular belief, you don't need a high income to afford the ability to travel or live abroad. The most important rule is, logically, that your costs are less than your income.

Whether you structure your travels and budget around a fixed income or aim for an income based on your preferred lifestyle and budget needs, the end equation remains the same.

TJ Lee, a travel vlogger and photographer, wrote a post about money management, travel costs, and budgeting for people curious about how to travel for a year. Her advice about how to approach spending is honest and on point, though accumulating debt to pay for your lifestyle shouldn't be part of your strategy at all as a digital nomad:

> *I'm going to say something that you'll hate. Don't drop everything to travel if you haven't been diligently paying off your debts OR if you don't have a plan to pay some off during the trip.*
>
> *Boom. I hate being the bearer of bad news but it's so important to travel responsibly. Why am I saying this? Because during the year you'll be like this :)!! And then when you return you'll be like this :'((worrying about the ample amount of debt you've accumulated with the interests of a*

whole year. Money will also began to stress you out as you
travel, which is the surest way to ruin your experience.

TJ LEE

In order to work out your new monthly budget, you'll need to first consider several main factors, and then determine how you'll restructure your budget from what it is now at home to what it will be on the road.

Will the overall total remain the same or is a primary goal to spend less than you currently do? Will you be cutting costs across all categories of your current daily and monthly expenses, or reducing "rent" while adding in new expenses for travel and activities?

Determining how much you'll be spending is a chicken-or-egg question that is tied to where you'll be living, and we dive more into how to choose where to go in the *Location Scouting* chapter, but your overall budget should be a fixed constraint that guides all other choices.

- **Region and likely cities**: Where you are going to spend most of your time? For example, South East Asia is much cheaper than the United States or Europe.
- **Duration and Frequency of Travel:** How long will you stay and how often will you move around? It is often easier to negotiate prices for monthly apartment rates. Many digital nomads rent out a home base for a month or more at a time and then take short trips nearby instead of completely moving every time.
- **Food**: Eating is a major part of experiencing a new culture. Where and what will you eat? Are you more interested in cheap local eats or fine dining? Is working out of cafes and enjoying a nice coffee part of your

lifestyle and work approach? Do you enjoy cooking? If your apartment has a kitchen, you should be able to manage a smaller food budget if you prepare some meals at home.

- **Entertainment**: How will you spend your free time? Are drinking and socializing frequent activities and expenses for you? Do you like to find free events or frequently attend activities that cost $5-20 each? Will you be doing weekend trips or big ticket adventure experiences (like getting PADI scuba certified or hiking Machu Picchu), and if so, how much will you allocate to that each month?

We'll talk more about the ways you can spend your free time in the *Lifestyle* and *Local Culture* chapters, but you'll need to know what you can afford beforehand.

It Adds Up

There are many expenses that occur during travel and expat living beyond the four categories noted above that you might not account for at home but add up once you leave (or are costs you think might not follow you abroad... but they can!).

- **Fees:** Visas ($25 - $250 per country), baggage fees for airlines (sometimes at insane rates), ATM fees ($2-10/withdrawal)
- **Laundry:** Some apartments come with washing machines, but at hotels and rentals, you'll choose between sending laundry out to get washed (typically $1-3/lb) or find a launderette to DIY it (still costs something, though).

- **Transportation:** Whether it's tuktuks ($1-3/ride), public transport ($1-5/ride), or uber/cabs ($1-15+/ride), getting around can add up (looking at you, London!).
- **Medical:** Insurance (travel and medical) costs can range from minimal to high depending on what you want and need; you never know what medical needs (emergency and routine) might come up on the road or need to be taken care of if you're away from home long-term; some countries require vaccines and other medical preventions that can be quite expensive (some shots are $150 each); plus, of course, any of your own personal prescriptions, devices, and other anticipated needs.
- **Giving and Getting:** You will want and need to buy new goods, clothes, and electronics for yourself, and you may want to buy gifts and souvenirs for friends and family, so budget for both recreational and required spending on shopping. When traveling, we also often encounter situations and people that inspire us to make a difference or help people in need, so you may want to budget for donations to charities and positive impact organizations. (You may also want to account for volunteer time in your schedule and routine.)
- **Back Home:** While you may have wrapped up most things back home before leaving, something usually crops up, whether it's paying for storage, dealing with unexpected natural disasters, unfortunate family events or illness - life back home can still affect you on the road. It's better to expect to spend time and money resolving those than be thrown completely off course when it happens.

Cost of Living: The Varying Price of a Beer Will Shock You

A typical pilsner in Prague might cost you 50 cents, but in Singapore, it could be 15 dollars. Do your research on what standard items in a country or city might cost in order to accurately build your budget.

One of the most complete databases of city cost-of-living is Numbeo. Researching potential cities and comparing their average housing, food, and transportation costs can give you a good idea of where you can easily live within your budget, what's a stretch, and where you can't (yet) go. (We dive into how to do this in the *Location Scouting* chapter.)

Once you have a shortlist of interesting places to you, and their respective general costs, drill down further to locate areas within the cities that are more affordable as that will dictate your daily expenses with housing and nearby food options. (We will discuss ways to find your new home in the *Housing* chapter.)

Food is often the second largest monthly cost, and one that can get out of hand quickly if you don't monitor your spending. If you are on a tighter budget, it'll be good to make sure your accommodation has a kitchen, with at least a range and fridge.

You'll still likely eat out some, and you should taste the local cuisine, so ensure that you budget accordingly. Interestingly, in some places eating out can be just as affordable as staying home. Street carts and food stalls in Asia typically sell dishes for $1-3 since they have low cost ingredients and economy of scale on their side.

Be realistic with yourself - you'll likely want to socialize with new friends (or go out and meet people), so budget for drinks and social activities. In some countries, beer is cheaper than water (Eastern Europe), whereas in other places alcohol is considerably more expensive than average (Indonesia). Prices at nightclubs typically mimic western prices, so keep that in mind as well.

You'll need at least a month of expenses saved in case of emergencies. We have found that, when calculating your costs for the month, adding an extra 20% as padding on top of what you think you'll spend is the safest way to go. It's hard to account for absolutely everything, and if you can't afford the extra padding then you should save more money before traveling, or pick a more affordable location or place to live.

> Katherine Says:
>
> *Keep track of your money! I am a huge nerd about spreadsheets and money tracking, and I think it makes such a big difference.*
>
> *I personally have to carefully track my money to stay within my budget, but it's worth it because I am also intent on balancing enjoying the city, having new experiences, and eating all the things.*

There are also several online applications you can use to help you keep track of your money, spending, and trends. Mint is one of the most popular ones, and it can email you weekly summaries of your spending categories as well as export out a spreadsheet. Personal Capital is another similar service.

Signing up for one of these can help you be more mindful of your money, though they do require connection to your bank and credit card accounts, which is a security consideration for some.

Sample Remote Year Budget

Katherine Says:

My digital nomad lifestyle + financial strategy is keeping overall costs down while indulging in a few things I enjoy and value.

I eat out approximately 1-2x a day, drink cappuccinos while working in nice cafes, do 1-3 side trips or major activities each month, only go out / drink alcohol a couple times a week, and typically walk to my workspace.

KATHERINE'S REMOTE YEAR involved 12 months spent in 12 cities + countries (Montevideo, Buenos Aires, La Paz, Cusco, London, Prague, Belgrade, Split, Kuala Lumpur, Koh Phangan, Phnom Penh, and Ho Chi Minh City), so these expenses reflect the average across South America, Europe, and SE Asia over a year.

Below is a summary of Katherine's **actual** average expenses (in USD) on Remote Year. This does **not** include any personal, insurance, medical, taxes, gifts, donations, or home expenses (like storage).

- Remote Year (Accommodation, Monthly Travel, Workspace, Events, Staff Support): $2000 / month, $27,000 total for the year
- Additional Travel: $200-500 / month
- Food: $400-600 / month
- Activities: $100-300 / month
- Social: $50-150 / month
- Transportation: $50-100 / month
- Work: $100-150 / month
- **Total: $2900 - 4000 / month**

In the *Digital Nomad Tool Kit* at the end, we've included additional guidance on how to budget for your lifestyle as a digital nomad (or otherwise!).

What's In Your Wallet?

There are several key factors you need to be aware of when making purchases overseas. Many credit and debit cards charge a foreign transaction fee, meaning that any purchase done outside your country of residence results in an additional percentage fee (usually 3% of the transaction). While this fee may not seem large, it can add up quickly over many charges, and it can result in hundreds of dollars of fees over the course of a month.

However, there are credit cards that offer zero percent foreign transaction fees. In the United States, one of many options is Chase's Sapphire Preferred credit card (or their new Sapphire Reserve card), which offers other benefits that are particularly traveler-friendly.

Making purchases on your credit card also gives you protection against fraud and often results in a better exchange rate than money exchange or withdrawing cash. However, you will not always have the ability to use a card, especially in many developing countries.

You should always have backup cash with you. To be able to get cash at a bank or cash machine, you should have one (and one backup) bank card. You will find that the fees at the machine will quickly add up - one fee to the cash machine operators, and one to your bank. In some places, it's possible to pay over $10 for withdrawing $100 worth of local currency - which adds an invisible 10% cost to anything you purchase with that cash.

Many US Citizens use Charles Schwab's checking account and bank card because they don't charge any fees and also reimburse any additional ATM / cash machine fees that you've been charged, automatically credited back to your account at the end of each month. This saves many digital nomads hundreds of dollars a year in fees. Schwab also seems to be good about sending replacement cards abroad in the case of a loss. Research if your country has a bank with similar perks and get the account set up before you leave.

For EU residents, Revolut is a common financial solution because they offer free ATM withdrawals up to 500 euros per month globally, as well as free international transfers between accounts in your name. They also offer a mobile app to conveniently monitor spending.

We reached out to Revolut and asked a few questions about how they see and serve digital nomads. (Note: we do not have any partnership or relationship with Revolut.)

What financial difficulties could arise from becoming a digital nomad?

Traditional banks underserve individuals who lead a global lifestyle. It takes weeks to open a bank account abroad; there's huge costs to spend or transfer money globally; onerous overdraft charges and clunky mobile apps. Banking simply hasn't caught up with the 21st Century's digital, globalised society.

Digital nomads face considerable fees to use their money abroad. Our recent survey of four major UK banks found that customers were charged on average £47 in exchange rate markups and transaction fees to spend £500 in Europe.* These costs are rarely transparent to the consumer.

*Our survey of HSBC, Natwest, RBS and Lloyds Bank was carried out on 14 December 2016. We assumed 50% ATM withdrawal and 50% card payments.

Has Revolut considered digital nomads as a demographic that would benefit from your products?

The digital nomad is precisely who Revolut is designed for. Revolut was born from a common frustration with opaque fees and the overall hassle of managing a bank account abroad.

What future plans do you have to help frequent travelers with their finances?

Our new spending analytics tool currently in the App maps out how much you've spent in each country and at which merchant. Perfect for nomads on a shoe-string budget!

With the upcoming introduction of unique customer IBANs (International Bank Account Number), freelancers and digital nomads alike will be able to pay their salaries directly into their Revolut account. We also plan to release 12 additional top-up currencies in 2017.

International transfers between banks using different currencies can incur hefty fees, something your clients may not like very much when paying your invoices.

Transferwise, "a peer-to-peer money transfer service" with lower transfer costs, comes well recommended by digital nomads citing their fee transparency as a more affordable option than traditional bank wires.

Be Practical with Plastic

Credit cards can be an extremely useful and beneficial tool as a traveler, but you should never, ever spend money you don't have. So while there are many advantages of having at least one credit card, it's only a good idea if you are responsible with your money.

- **Backup Cards + Cash**: It's a good idea to have a debit and credit card in your daily wallet, and one or two of each in your locked safe in your housing. It is often very difficult (and sometimes impossible) to get replacement cards sent to your address when abroad. Keep an extra stash of cash (local and USD) locked in a safe (when available) in case of wallet theft.
- **Travel Points**: Since you are likely buying many airline or train tickets, as well as hotels or Airbnbs, it would be a good idea to get a credit card that gives you points or cash back on travel. Make sure to sign up for every airline frequent flier / mileage program that you buy tickets for (though double check whether partner airlines let you use other programs), and it may help to use a co-branded credit card to earn additional points.
- **Travel Perks**: Research additional perks that come with your travel loyalty programs or credit cards. Sometimes, you will get complimentary travel insurance on flights, as well as rental car insurance if you ever need to rent a car. There are also cards that give reimbursement stipends, as well as trip cancellation or delay reimbursements as well. Research what benefits different cards offer to figure out what is most useful for your needs and lifestyle.
- **Sign-up Bonuses**: If you are a financially solvent individual, you can get free or discounted flights by using a bank's credit card signup bonuses to your advantage. Be careful that you are paying off the balance in full every month, or else you will find yourself in debt quickly.
- **ATM / Cash Machine Limits**: If your card or PIN is ever compromised, having a limit on the total amount of purchases or cash withdrawals in a day can help hedge

your losses in these situations. Also, keeping your main checking account card locked at home, and a cash-machine-only card with you in your wallet can also keep your savings safe against thieves. Always better to be safe than sorry.

Taxation and Location

Taxes are an important thing to consider as a digital nomad as you might not owe as much thanks to being out of your home country for the majority of the year. And regardless of whether you save money, becoming a digital nomad may impact your tax status at home, so researching this is a critical point of setting up your new lifestyle.

Again, we are not financial experts and this book is not a substitute for any professional advice, whether financial, legal, health related, or otherwise. Please consult an accountant to ensure you file your taxes accurately.

US Citizens

In our unofficial and non-expert opinions, most US citizens should be able to claim the FEIE as digital nomads, assuming you meet the requirements of the physical presence test:

> *Generally, to meet the physical presence test, you must be physically present in a foreign country or countries for at least 330 full days during the 12-month period. You can count days you spent abroad for any reason. You do not have to be in a foreign country only for employment purposes. You can be on vacation time.*
> [Foreign Earned Income Exclusion]

The physical presence test is one of two ways (the other being the bona fide residence test) to qualify for FEIE, and both have strict and specific requirements in order to make the claim without issue.

The IRS's publication 54 has all the information about it, and though dense, does explain and give examples about all the factors of filing and possible inclusions / exclusions. [IRS Pub. 54]

However, challenges aside, it can be extremely beneficial to your finances, so it's worth the research - for managing your finances and taxes as well as planning your days spent abroad and at home.

FEIE results in an exemption, i.e.: negative income, so the benefit of claiming is that you pay no or less federal income tax. Here's a very broad example to illustrate how much you could save that, of course, is heavily dependent on meeting specific requirements and your exact situation. (Please do consult a professional.)

FEIE Example:

Say you go abroad on February 1, 2016 and do not return to the United States that year, so by the end of 2016, you will have spent 335 days abroad, fulfilling the 330 minimum requirement for the FEIE physical presence test (see details about travel dates and rules).

Your maximum exclusion is 335/365 = 91.7% of $101,300 (the max limit for 2016), so 91.7% ($101,300) = $92,973 possible excluded income.

So if you earned less than $92k in income, you would *probably* not have to pay any federal income tax. If you earned more than $92k, then you'd pay income tax on the amount over (for $100k, you'd pay tax on the $8k over, at the $100k tax rate).

In a normal year (not filing FEIE), say you'd pay 20% in federal taxes, so you would owe $20,000 of your $100,000 *income. With FEIE, in this rough example, you'd pay the 20% tax only on the $8,000 difference, so you'd only owe $1,600 instead.*

This example is obviously not specific or accurate, but it illustrates the possible benefit of claiming FEIE if possible.

However, of course, if you do not qualify for FEIE, you would still owe taxes, so before you change how your taxes are withheld, please talk to an accountant about how to set this up so you do not owe taxes later or incur a penalty.

If you are freelance/self-employed, regardless of FEIE, you still have to pay your 15.3% self-employment taxes. Another ridiculously simple example:

Say you are a self-employed consultant and will qualify for FEIE. Your foreign earned income is $50,000, your business deductions are $10,000, so your net profit is $40,000.

You will have to pay your 15.3% self-employment taxes on the $40,000 net profit, which would equal $6,120.

Careful! Apparently there are very strict restrictions about claiming this and being able to contribute to your IRAs, among other things, if claiming FEIE. Double check with your accountant about how to handle your savings or retirement plans.

You can (and should) talk to your regular accountant (if you have one) about filing, but don't be discouraged if they aren't sure at first. It's still a relatively uncommon filing, so they may need to do more research, or you may need to work with expat tax professionals who specialize in helping people file their 1040 federal income tax return as well as the additional forms + schedules to claim FEIE and maximize your savings.

Travel Insurance: Prepare for the Worst

When traveling abroad, there are many ways to take precautions against injury and theft, but you may still encounter unfortunate situations - whether it's a broken ankle in Southeast Asia or salmonella poisoning in South America, a snatched purse off a restaurant chair in Rome or an apartment burglary in Buenos Aires.

There are many financial risks that come with traveling, working remotely, and staying abroad long-term. Travel insurance is one way to protect yourself financially from consequences of loss, theft, and repair of your technology and belongings as well as healthcare expenses.

There are several insurance providers for digital nomads, and you should compare the plans and costs accordingly. Plan variables include maximum limit, deductible, "enhanced accidental death and dismemberment" coverage, and length of coverage. If you are planning to do anything "extreme," like surfing, skiing, motorbiking - you may need to upgrade your plan to include this in advance.

World Nomads is an insurance specifically targeted at independent travelers, whereas other large insurance brands, like IMG, offer short-term travel and medical plans.

There are many insurance providers and coverage options available, so research the one that best fits your travel plans, destinations, budget, health concerns, and comfort level. (We discuss device insurance more in the *Technology* chapter.)

Nomad Census Results: Monthly Budgets

In our research for *The Digital Nomad Survival Guide*, we surveyed almost 200 digital nomads and asked about their spending habits on housing, entertainment, and food to get a better picture of how much people were spending in various locations around the world.

Our research confirms the common idea that Thailand is one of the cheapest locations, so it's no wonder it was also the most popular destination amongst digital nomads. The USA was a popular location for nomads in the survey, and although it can be an expensive proposition in certain cities, that doesn't mean the entire US is prohibitively expensive.

Ultimately, with proper budgeting and planning, you can live wherever you please.

Key Takeaways: Finances

- Your financial situation, such as your income per month, will determine where you can live and what type of housing arrangement. Do your research on cost-of-living before planning your destinations.
- Research and acquire the right bank accounts and credit cards before starting your travels.
- Create a detailed budget for your year or anticipated travel time (at least the first few months), estimating your daily and monthly costs for housing, travel, food, entertainment, work, and other expenses you plan to incur.
- Keep track of your income and expenses for at least your first few months to see how sustainable your spending habits are.

LOCATION SCOUTING

"Where's the best place for me to live as a digital nomad?"

ONCE YOU HAVE a handle on your financial situation and anticipated budget, you can begin making your travel plans. Whether it's a place you'll call home for two weeks or two years, having the freedom to choose where to live – out of all the cities in the world – is one of the most exciting and rewarding aspects of being a digital nomad.

Bangkok, Bali, Buenos Aires, or Budapest: the choice is yours. But how do you choose?

Home is Where the ___ Is

By location scouting, we aren't referring to finding a great place to shoot the next Star Wars film, we're talking about doing your due diligence for your first nomadic basecamp.

In the self-assessment, you reflected on many aspects of both the digital nomad experience that appeals to you as well as other factors in your personal and work life that need to be taken into account.

Ensuring that you have a clear understanding of what you need (and what you don't) is critical to setting yourself up for success. To sustain the digital nomad lifestyle, it's important to put yourself in a location and environment where you're happy and productive.

This isn't to suggest you stay within the same comforts of home and only in familiar environments. Plus, a major draw of this lifestyle is stepping outside your world and into a new one.

But understanding your dealbreakers *and* learning how to adapt are both key to having a rewarding and long-term lifestyle as a digital nomad.

For your first location, in particular, it's wise to choose somewhere that will set a positive tone for the experience and allow you to transition effectively. As you adjust to your new lifestyle, you can better identify your future needs as well as where you can push yourself outside your current comfort zone.

The idea is to start in a place where your enthusiasm for your new lifestyle can shift into momentum to continue it through the challenging days, weeks, and months that will inevitably come. The honeymoon period will end (because this really is still "real life," even if it looks different), and if you want to make this a long-term lifestyle, you'll want to start with a solid foundation.

Define what you want out of the nomadic experience. Is it a home for several months or even a year? Or are you looking for many different locations during a month's time?

Make your list of all the qualifications of an ideal location and daily lifestyle.

Parameters of a Place

The basics of finding a good nomadic location is a similar process to choosing a holiday destination – and to the pre-production process of finding a spot for a photo or video shoot. That's why we call it location scouting!

First, you have to define the rubric you'll use to evaluate destinations.

Weather

What is your ideal climate? What seasons do you enjoy - and what weather makes you miserable? Part of the benefit of living where you want is living there *when* you want. You can help ensure the reality will match your imagination if you plan to be somewhere during the season you're excited to experience.

Be sure to check the weather report and the general climate of the city or region to ensure you're likely to land during a pleasant period - and don't forget that seasons are flipped on the other side of the equator. January in New York may be freezing while Rio will be blazing hot.

Southeast Asia and India have monsoon and rainy seasons just as Europe and North America have white winters. Both can impact your daily activities or significantly affect travel and lifestyle options.

You'll also need to determine whether you'll be planning to "follow summer" (or another season) or live in ranging climates because that will impact your packing list. Prioritizing certain climates (warmer ones in particular) can reduce the volume and weight of your luggage significantly.

Wikipedia offers high-level summaries of climate data for cities and countries, and ClimateList offers an interactive tool and comparison between different locations in different months.

Politics and Current Events

The political climate and activities in regions and cities can impact both travel plans and daily life, so it's important to take that into account.

Peter says:

We have a good example of how political climates in regions can affect travel plans. On our original Remote Year itinerary, Istanbul was one of our destinations for a month of the year.

Istanbul is a wonderful, historic city to visit, and many people were excited to live there. It's rich in culture, beautiful landscapes, and delicious foods, but when we started our Remote Year, the political situation was looking unstable.

Based on consultations from outside experts and internal assessments, the Remote Year management team decided not to send our group there, changing that month's location to London.

With the conflict in Syria only one border away, it wasn't safe or reasonable to bring 70 international tourists in one big group to the city, all of whom are actively publishing their locations and activities to social media.

We were disappointed to miss Istanbul, but London had different things to offer as a month-long home. And at the end of June 2016, mere days before our originally scheduled departure from Istanbul, several terrorists detonated a bomb in the airport terminal, killing several civilians. It was a scary and sad moment for Istanbul and the world, and it proved the need to put safety first.

While it's wonderful to challenge your comfort zones while exploring the world, know what is reasonable for you. There's always a balance when traveling in knowing what is safe, what is manageable given certain precautions, and what is too risky.

For US Citizens, you can register with the Smart Traveler Enrollment Program:

The Smart Traveler Enrollment Program (STEP) is a free service to allow U.S. citizens and nationals traveling abroad to enroll their trip with the nearest U.S. Embassy or Consulate. Benefits of Enrolling in STEP:

- *Receive important information from the Embassy about safety conditions in your destination country, helping you make informed decisions about your travel plans.*

- *Help the U.S. Embassy contact you in an emergency, whether natural disaster, civil unrest, or family emergency.*
- *Help family and friends get in touch with you in an emergency.*

On the other hand, it's important to balance those fears and risks with knowing the reality of the world - anywhere.

We feel comfortable and confident in our home environment, but it may not actually be measurably safer than foreign cities and countries. Perhaps we simply know how to avoid unsafe situations or areas at home, or it's the unfamiliarity that we fear.

Learning about the local culture and common challenges means you can often adapt to a reasonably safe lifestyle in what may initially seem like an overwhelming or risky environment.

This is why research is key – know the facts and stats, understand the current political climate, be realistic about what is part of international travel, and define where to draw the line for your safety.

Connectivity

Knowing what you need to work is key to keeping yourself productive and your lifestyle sustainable. Determine your bandwidth requirements, and then evaluate internet and cellular data options for the countries and cities to decide where you can (or can't) work.

It's always important to check the average internet upload and download speeds as your ability to have video calls and manage work files will be critical to your professional success as a nomad.

Pro Tip:

There is a handy Wikipedia entry that ranks each country's speeds, which you can use as a starting point for identifying good destinations.

Working Requirements

Beyond the bandwidth issue, you should consider the type of work environment you need and enjoy – and not everyone wants to (or can) be on a beach with their laptop.

Certain cities and locations may have coworking spaces that offer the amenities of an office and a more professional environment, which can be beneficial from a productivity and social perspective.

In others, you may be working out of cafes, or the only viable option could be your accommodations.

Think through where and how you like to work and what your technical needs are, then use that to evaluate where you can live (and where you may want to visit during slow periods or holiday seasons).

Access

Depending on how often you'll be changing locations as well as taking "side trips," you may need to choose easily accessible places only – or you may be able to live in more remote areas.

If you plan on staying put for weeks or months at a time, it may not matter and you might enjoy the relative isolation of a smaller island, for example. However, you may want to live in a hub city to take advantage of frequent day or weekend trips, or you may want to move on a more frequent basis but have shorter travel days.

Another access consideration is whether you'll be hosting or meeting up with other travelers and visitors. If you're persuading family to come for the holidays, you'll likely want to position yourself somewhere they can afford to visit in an allotted amount of time.

Identify what your radius needs to be from airports, train and bus stations, ports, and other transportation hubs to see what destinations are doable for you, and note how and when certain times of year can affect those requirements.

Friends & Family

You may be enticed to visit and live in locations where you know people. This is an excellent way to find a destination to start in, and having that "safety net" can help you overcome the initial inertia of picking a place and making such a big change.

However, as you become more acclimated to perpetual travel, consider traveling solo and venturing to new-to-you (and your network) places. Being in a new environment on your own can be insightful and allow you to improve and grow as a person. It also allows (or forces) you to find ways to meet new people and establish new relationships.

Katie McKnoulty, a veteran digital nomad and blogger, makes an important point about solo travel as an integral part of nomadic lifestyles:

> *It'll feel crap for a little while maybe but you'll get over it...*
> *That's the best feeling in the world for a nomad I think,*
> *personal growth, and it often comes from putting yourself in*
> *situations where you're completely alone.*

> KATIE MCKNOULTY

Being vulnerable is a scary feeling, and we tend to make most life decisions to actively avoid it. But it's also where we find personal growth, and becoming a digital nomad is often about more than being able to work from anywhere - it's about discovering more about who you are and who you want to become.

Incorporating some solo travel is often a critical part of that self-discovery process. It also encourages you to fulfill your ambitions for adventure as well as meet new friends and grow your network.

Culture & Community

Interacting with and observing a different culture is an exciting part of being a digital nomad, and while it's generally positive to encounter new things, it's helpful to plan the cultural environment and type of community you want to live in.

The chapters on *Lifestyle* and *Local Culture* dive into that more from a social perspective, but it's good to keep in mind what culture you can and want to live and work in when figuring out where you want to go.

Are you trying to practice a certain language? Do you have strong dietary restrictions or preferences? Are you curious about specific cultures? Do you enjoy certain outdoor activities or want to live in a particular geographic region?

It's important to consider both culture and community from a local as well as a digital nomad and expat perspective. Different cities and locations may be easier to integrate into quickly while others may require longer to understand and find your footing in. You may want to be around an obvious and accessible expat / digital nomad community, or you might want to find somewhere less popular or populated.

Destination Hotspots

You are certain to find some remote workers in all corners of the globe, and you may either seek out digital nomad hotspot or prefer to avoid some of the more popular ones if you are looking for a more local feel.

However, as many people are interested in networking with other like-minded folks as well as gaining a sense of community, you may want to research some of the places below (or some of the many others that weren't able to be included in this book) to weave into your itinerary.

(We also outline formal digital nomad program options in the *Housing* chapter.)

Nomad Favorites

Chiang Mai, Thailand

Chiang Mai is considered the most popular digital nomad location, largely due to the cost of living. HSBC Bank's expat survey ranked it as the most affordable city for foreigners to make a second home.

Because of the influx of travelers entering the area, the internet is often very reliable, and many co-working and co-living arrangements have sprung up.

Michael Hullman, author of the guide to Chiang Mai titled "Digital Nomad Escape Plan" writes that these factors make "Chiang Mai a petri dish of collaboration and innovation with new ideas being conceptualized and created at coffee shops and coworking spaces around the city everyday."

If you value being around a plethora of similarly-minded folks, and the idea of a "Thailand Silicon Valley" appeals to you, you may want to head straight to Chiang Mai.

> **Pros**: Popular with digital nomads, many cafes and coworking spaces, affordable

> **Cons**: Busy with tourists, expats, and other digital nomads; watch out for spring burning season

Bali, Indonesia

Bali is a nomad haven for those who want to live a more alternative lifestyle and be in a scenic location. There are many areas of the island to choose from, each with their share of nomads wandering around, as well as being host to other travellers on holiday.

Canggu and Seminyak areas are great for those who surf or enjoy beaches, while Ubud is the more nomad-dense area with great food in rich forests.

Internet speeds are good but not great, so getting a powerful LTE SIM-card can help you connect everywhere you go.

> **Pros**: Many different locations to explore, beaches, healthy lifestyle
>
> **Cons**: Internet connection can be slower than ideal; very popular destination

Lisbon, Portugal

In the words of Tiago, a friend from Lisbon:

> *To me, living the nomadic life means having good wifi in a cheap place with great weather, and Portugal is definitely the place to be. I'm not staying it because I'm from there but because I travel so I now appreciate my country.*
>
> *Portugal is one of the cheapest countries in Europe. We are a poor country with a minimum wage of just over $600, but we have amazing telecommunication systems. Wifi is pretty good everywhere and you can get 4G SIM cards for a cheap price.*
>
> *Portuguese people are proud of their food for a reason as it's super tasty and with always good wine around. We got pretty much the best weather compared to other European countries as well as a beautiful coast facing the ocean. All of these factors together sum up in a pretty good lifestyle for a digital nomad to settle.*

Lisbon is the capital and tourism industry is booming lately and a top choice for this lifestyle. Porto is another city in the north that is getting a lot of attention as well (and is my favorite).

Barrio Alto is the place to be, for many reasons. There are plenty of cafes around where you can work from and this is where nightlife starts. Hit Rua cor-de-rosa (Pink street) to find out what I'm talking about!

Regarding accommodations you can probably get a nice place for $600 monthly. Food is cheap, and there are literally mini-markets in every corner! Lisbon is a great start especially if you are into water sports as surf is a big scene here. If you want to get more cultural, check out Porto!

Pros: Affordable European country, good internet, good food, nice weather

Cons: Popular tourist destination, more expensive than other nomad destinations, late night party culture, locals are not always very English-fluent, can be dangerous at night

Budapest, Hungary

Budapest is a location that is emerging as a new European hot spot for digital nomads. Infrastructure is evolving across the city: new tram lines and new apartment complexes, and Budapest offers affordable cost-of-living in terms of food and housing. A two bedroom apartment in the city-center is often under $600, which makes it quite affordable if you have a roommate.

Nomads who have ventured to Budapest recommend using Facebook as the means to find short or long term housing, and a source recommends anywhere in the city center, except for District

8. Be careful in the winter - if you are not a fan of the cold you may want to look elsewhere.

As with other parts of eastern Europe, beer can be cheaper than water, which makes a night out less expensive, and Budapest is centrally located to other great travel destinations, such as the beaches and boats of Croatia, the vineyards of Vienna, and the party barges in Belgrade.

> **Pros**: Emerging economy, good internet, and lots of history and culture to immerse yourself into
>
> **Cons**: Cold winters, landlocked

While there are many popular and familiar destinations for digital nomads, don't discount off-the-radar locations.

For example, while it may not be suitable for everyone, some nomads have had success working and traveling through Iran given the booming tech scene that has sprouted up in Tehran.

Adil Ghereb wrote a guide article of Iran for MatadoreNetwork.com, in which he says that some cities in Iran have many coworking spaces or other places to get solid wifi. "You can try to negotiate an office space at one of the three startup incubators in Tehran: Avatech, DMOND or MAPS."

While Iran may not suit everyone's tastes due to the more-strict social and cultural norms, this is one example of how nomad-friendly places can be somewhere you least expect and "ideal" destinations vary from person to person.

Not Quite Nomad Friendly

Nomads are less likely to live in higher cost-of-living cities and countries, and sometimes factors like language, climate, cultural, or dietary challenges make a destination better for visiting (or finding a local job) than for working remotely.

A few examples of cities and countries that nomads tend avoid:

- **Japan**: Ultimately, as culturally rich as a country as Japan is, it's more difficult to achieve sustainability due to higher housing and food prices, as well as low English penetration.
- **San Francisco**: While there are many people in tech here, and it's somewhere that offers excellent internet, the housing market is too competitive to be affordable for most digital nomads.
- **Bolivia**: La Paz was previously on the list of the Remote Year program cities (we were one of two groups that spent a month there); however, the unstable internet conditions and health challenges (food, water, and altitude) made it less than ideal for working remotely. While there are plenty of amazing things to do and see in Bolivia, it may be somewhere to visit rather than attempt to live and work remotely from.

Research Resources

Note: These are also compiled in the *Digital Nomad Tool Kit* at the end along with our other recommendation + reference links.

- **Numbeo** is the world's largest database of user-contributed data about cities and countries worldwide. Numbeo provides current and timely information on world living conditions including cost of living, housing indicators, health care, traffic, crime and pollution.
- **Wikipedia** typically offers high-level summaries of climate data for cities and countries on their

individual Wiki pages. Wikipedia also has a list of countries by internet speeds.

- **Ookla Speedtest** puts the most sophisticated broadband testing and analysis tools into the hands of anyone interested in finding out just how connected they actually are. This free service from Ookla opens hundreds of testing locations around the world to anyone curious about the performance of their Internet connection. http://www.speedtest.net/
- **ClimateList** helps you visualize when is the best time to travel. ClimateList.com
- **Teleport:** "Tell us what matters to you and we'll recommend great places to live. Teleport Cities finds your best places to be in the world, based on how your personal preferences match 254 cities around the world." https://teleport.org/
- **Destigogo:** "We bring you the best travel destinations that truly fit within your budget. We hand-curated 650+ of world's best travel destinations, examined thousands of flight- and hotel prices and collected tons of additional information." https://destigogo.com/
- **NomadList** finds you the best places in the world to live and work remotely. https://nomadlist.com/
- **Digital Nomads Around the World (Facebook group):** This is a place for digital nomads to share advice and tips related to living the digital nomad lifestyle. Sharing our experiences and knowledge can only be a good thing! :)

Stay Organized

Outline your preferences, and consider making a rubric so you know what items are must-haves versus negotiables.

Once you start doing your research, figure out which application (Trello, Google Docs, a spreadsheet, notes, etc) allows you to record your research of different locations. (We have a list of organizational tools and apps in the *Digital Nomad Tool Kit*.)

It's helpful to keep track of both the locations you are interested in as well as ones you think you'll want to avoid, and you'll want to note key variables and data points for each for easy comparison and future planning.

Key Takeaways: Location Scouting

- Define your must-have list for your digital nomad destinations (considering personal preferences, work needs, climate, travel, and other factors).
- Research locations that meet your top requirements.
- Review nomad hotspots and compare with your priorities and needs to determine which you may want to visit and when.
- Find a system to organize your research and keep track of potential options.

HOUSING

"What are the best resources to find housing while traveling as a digital nomad?"

YOU'VE NOW HOPEFULLY SETTLED on a location for your nomadic start, or at least a shortlist of destinations. Finding housing can feel like one of the more difficult challenges, and how to do it well is a question that comes up often when new nomads are starting out.

However, it can actually be an enjoyable process. Finding the sweet spot between location, affordability, and amenities can be a fun optimization challenge for those of us with analytical minds.

You Can Use a Middle Man

Over the last few years, given the increasing appeal of the digital nomad lifestyle, there are companies popping up that offer to handle logistics for you, so that essentially all you need to do is show up.

Their fees typically are higher than it would cost to travel on your own, but the benefits of saving your time and using their expertise and resources can make it worth it.

With any agent or program, keep in mind that you're subjecting yourself to someone else's standards, not your own. You should expect to receive reasonable standards of service and accommodations for your fees, but their rubric may differ from your own. They're working to negotiate and book housing and travel that make sense for the group as a whole. Be realistic about whether that's something that can work for you.

Obviously, they're aiming for customer satisfaction, and they have teams dedicated to setting up everything for the group and keeping things running smoothly. These programs can be beneficial for new and experienced nomads alike, depending on if you're ready for less logistics responsibility or more community facilitation.

If you are reading this book and have signed up for a program, then great! You have one less thing to worry about when planning your daily lifestyle. However, the information in this chapter is still useful for any independent travel you may do, such as weekend trips, or your future lifestyle as a solo digital nomad.

Digital Nomad Programs + Companies

Remote Year, currently the biggest and most established of these, started with one program in 2015 and now is up to 10 different cohorts of travelers. Remote Year's groups typically have 60-75 participants, and each program runs for 12 months, living in a different city every month. http://www.remoteyear.com/

Currently, participants pay $27,000 for the year, and in return, Remote Year provides them with a private bedroom (at minimum), access to a workspace, travel between each itinerary city, staff support, and some events.

Katherine says:

Because of our personal experience as participants on the program, Remote Year is the company we're most familiar with. As their second ever group, we were literally the beta testers. The year was a mix of highs and lows, which is to be expected in life, in travel, and with a new company.

It was an incredible year of travel, and it was really nice to have other people with me to explore the cities we lived in and go on side trips with. Doing it alone for 18 months beforehand made me appreciate their planning and my RY community a lot.

Certainly, there were areas that needed improvement and times (primarily early on) when RY did not appropriately deliver what they'd promised us in our contract. But, over the course of the year, most of that was rectified, and the program, experience, and support improved.

The benefits of having the majority of planning responsibilities taken off my plate plus bonding with my community made it a very worthwhile experience overall.

As the company, program, and experience continues to evolve, however, it's hard to translate exactly what a future experience might be based solely on our own.

For reference, Remote Year ran 6 programs in 2016, and they're planning to launch 12+ in 2017.

There were approximately 10-15 staff total with the company when we joined, and participant program fees were their only source of revenue (that I'm aware of). They have since announced a $12 million Series A funding (October 2016), and, as of January 2017, have around 100 employees.

A program is worth considering if the fees are within a feasible budget, you want to minimize planning time, you're willing to relinquish considerable control over many factors in your life, and engaging with a community long-term is important.

Other companies that also offer services like housing, travel, and/or community events for varying time periods and locations include:

- **Hacker Paradise**:Travel the world. Build cool things. Meet awesome people. We organize trips all over the world for developers, designers, and entrepreneurs who want to travel while working remotely or focusing on personal projects. http://www.hackerparadise.org/

- **Embark Together**: Embark brings together a talented community of entrepreneurs and creative professionals who work and travel together. We provide the community, accommodation, work space and transportation, so you can focus on what matters most to you. http://www.embarktogether.io/
- **Wifi Tribe**:Every month, we choose a different city to call home. We are inviting a mix of young, wild and free, location-independent professionals to join us anywhere along the way: entrepreneurs, photographers, developers, writers, designers, marketers, adventure addicts. http://wifitribe.co/
- **We Roam**: We are a travel-while-working program that curates trips around the world for select remote workers who want to pursue their love of travel, without putting their careers on hold. http://www.we-roam.com/
- **Terminal 3**:Terminal 3 is more than a vacation. It's your opportunity to savor local cuisines, connect with locals, make lifelong friends and find yourself in the process. And when you travel with us you make the world a better place by giving back to local communities. http://www.terminal3.co/
- **Roam**:Roam is a network of global coliving spaces that provide everything you need to feel at home and be productive the moment you arrive. Strong, battle-tested wifi, a coworking space, chef's kitchen and a diverse community. https://www.roam.co/

Wanted: More Than Just a Bed

As a digital nomad, you'll be looking for a place that fits both the needs of normal life while also providing some of the benefits of the location as a vacation destination. Typically, this is an apartment (or perhaps even a house) in a central yet quiet location, decent amenities, and good wifi all at affordable price.

There's always a possibility that you'll end up with less than ideal accommodation, and it can make productivity difficult and may impact your experience of living in that location. However, our advice should help minimize the risk of that happening, and with more experience, you'll develop a sense of what's real and what's too good to be true.

Those who are staying a month or longer usually use a different avenue for finding a location than someone who is only staying for a few days to a week. Additionally, a person's tolerance for noise, personal preferences for food and drink, among others all factor into the method of selection and areas that one would feel comfortable - just like searching for an apartment or flat back home.

Top Factors in Housing Location

- **Internet**: Check the reviews of hostels or hotels to see if they mention anything about bandwidth strength or concerns. Especially for hostels in areas that see a lot of digital nomad traffic, you may get some good leads. When courting a listing on Airbnb, you should always contact the owner first and can often get the owner to send a screenshot of a SpeedTest.net results before booking. For reference, Skype support documents say that in order to have a three-person video call, you need at least 2 Mbs download speed, and keep in mind that latency and consistency of the speed are important factors too.
- **Workspaces**: The density of new, reliable, and convenient places to work is a big factor in finding

housing. It would be inefficient to select a nice city that you want to explore, but then end up working from your apartment every day due to a lack of other options. Coffee shops with free wifi are often good places to work from, and you can allocate a portion of your work and food budget towards that expense. Look up local coworking spaces as they're often a good homebase for working, and they often provide opportunities for networking with other locals or nomads.

- **Transportation**: Research the available options for getting around, and consider whether you enjoy commuting and exploring a city on foot, biking, in cars, or via public transportation. Uber is increasingly available in foreign cities, and there are often other taxi apps in places where Uber isn't yet. If you can look at Uber in that city, see how many cars are on the roads to get an idea about whether you can live further from the city center. Depending on how long you'll be in that city and your comfort with driving a scooter, they're often available for short-term rentals to travelers in countries in SE Asia, for example. Regardless of the method of transportation you'll be using, it's a factor that will dictate where you can realistically live.

Example:

Say you have decided to spend three months in Buenos Aires, Argentina. You won't have a car, and you will have a regular need for Skype video calls. Through your research, you would learn that the Palermo Hollywood area has access to several co-working spaces as well as ample cafes with good wifi and lots of seating options. Public transport is a bit further away, but there is a lot within walking distance and Uber is newly available.

(Temporary) Home Hunting

Once you have finished the task of weighing the pros and cons of your destination, the next task is picking out a place. Luckily, this part can be more fun, as long as you have a strategy and set your expectations of how much time and energy you'll put into the search.

Thinking back to your self-assessment, what did you decide in terms of your priorities and budget? For example, is having a kitchen important to you in order to save money and eat healthy? Then you'll know whether you'll be looking for a hotel or apartment.

A good idea, regardless of the method, is to try to contact nomads or locals in the area and ask them about good neighborhoods, rental services or providers, and ways to find properties offline.

Reservation Services

Booking.com and Hostelworld are good for finding a hostel or guesthouse with a private room, decent internet connection, and in a good area. Because your job depends on expensive electronics, you'll want to invest in keeping them safe and yourself relaxed and rested. Reserve dorm-style arrangements for your side-trips or vacations to save money then if needed.

Couchsurfing is a website where users share their home for free with fellow travelers with the hope that they may be reciprocated in the future. While this may work for some travelers, it's not a good primary strategy for digital nomads and professionals. Ultimately, if you rely on free housing to make your lifestyle work, it's probably time to get a better paying job or restructure your approach. Couchsurfing's community can be a good way to network and meet people, though.

Airbnb is an excellent resource that is favored among many digital nomads, albeit being a bit more expensive compared to other options. Airbnb is a platform that allows local people to rent out either a couch/bed, a room in their home, or the entire flat to visitors who prefer staying in homes over hotels. It has become the go-to resource for many digital nomads, largely due to the fact that it helps travelers have a more local experience, makes it easy to find a unit with a kitchen, allows you to screen hosts and properties based on reviews, and payment is secured through the platform rather than made directly to the hosts with cash or your credit card.

Pro Tips: *Airbnb Strategies*

- Hosts often discount the rate for weekly or monthly stays, so make sure to look out for these listings (not all have this).
- While Airbnb is reputable as far as accuracy and accountability goes, it's still important to pay attention to the ratings and reviews. It's usually not recommended to book a place with no reviews. Also, if there are several reviews saying the host cancelled last minute, it may not a good idea to stay there because if it happened to someone else, it could happen to you.
- Don't forget to ask the host to send you a screenshot of an Internet speed test before you book to ensure you'll be able to have adequate bandwidth while there.
- If it's your first time using the service, you can get a discount on your first rental through the program. We've included a promo code in the Appendix of this book.
- If you're setting up a new account, you can connect to your friends on Airbnb and ask them to write a recommendation for you. While it's not the same as a

host's review, it helps validate that you're a real person and will be a good guest - because the evaluation process before booking at Airbnb is mutual.

In-Person Scouting

An approach that feels less secure and may require more effort is finding a place on the ground after arriving. Looking around on foot, you can often find monthly and longer rentals advertised locally - posted on the street, local websites, or via paper mailings.

This method requires some insider knowledge of how the housing market operates in an a given area, but it can result in great deals that aren't available online. Asian cities are better suited for local "analog" searches than European or American locations.

In an area like Bangkok, for example, there is a lot of housing supply for less demand, so prices can be very competitive compared to renting on Airbnb. Karsten Aichholz writes on his blog ThailandStarterKit.com about finding good locations on your own in Bangkok:

> *"Although things are moving more and more online, the best deals might be not be found on a website, especially when searching for information in English...*
>
> *That's where your real search for a deal starts: keep an eye open for apartment-for-rent signs in front of condo buildings, on doors of individual units and posted on streets nearby.*
>
> *If you can't read Thai, just take pictures with your phone of any sign listing a phone number and ask someone for help later on."*
>
> [An In-Depth Guide to Renting an Apartment in Bangkok]

Digital Nomad Community Housing

As mentioned about remote program options, there are now also housing options marketing themselves as digital nomad-friendly options with additional benefits outside the accommodations.

Roam.co offers nomads housing options in several cities around the world for one flat fee on month-to-month lease terms. Usually the fee includes a co-working desk membership as well as some community events, though that varies by location. http://roam.co/

Similarly, the company WeWork, who specialized in creating flexible coworking spaces around the US and internationally, has recently dipped their toe into co-living spaces. In their inaugural complex in New York City, they offer a private room for $1,900 or solo studio for around $3,000. It's expensive, so it does require income stability to be a viable option. https://www.wework.com/

In Wired.com's review of WeWork's NYC WeLive location, the author highlights the use of Silicon Valley-esque amenities around the space. "There's even a small concessions stand in the hallway, filled with toothpaste and tampons," Margaret Rhodes writes. "As is the case in WeWork offices, there's a certain kitschiness to some of WeLive's décor, like a poster in the hallway that reads 'Home is where your pants are off,' in splashy, brushstroke letters."

So while you may find co-living spaces to be on the more expensive side, they can often add a splash of luxury and community to your hectic life if you can afford it.

One of the more affordable co-living/co-working options is Startup House in San Francisco. Their accommodation package is usually below the market rate of the city's rentals. However, you'll find yourself in dorm-style living in an unattractive part of SF's SOMA district. But there are many nomads whose goal is to come to

Silicon Valley and make their dream of bootstrapping a startup a reality, so this can still appeal to a certain market. http://startuphouse.com/

Overall, it's important to evaluate prospective programs with a critical eye. These spaces are often created by professional marketers, branders, photographers, and editors. Their expertise is sales appeal, so they can make any space look attractive and sound like an amazing deal, even if the actual quality is below expectations. The promise of community events and group camaraderie may be more of a goal than a reality. Contact current residents and nomads who've lived there before to find out whether it will meet your needs.

Key Takeaways: Housing

- Do your homework! Research your location well in advance and make sure to check internet speeds and working locations as priorities.
- It's okay to go to a popular digital nomad hub for your first location, or to use a nomad housing arrangement to get your feet wet.
- Airbnb is a great way to easily get settled like a local in an unfamiliar place. Pay attention to their reviews!

TRAVEL & TRANSPORTATION

"What are the best ways to find flights to a new location?"

IF TECHNOLOGY IS one pillar of being a digital nomad, then traveling is the other. This chapter focuses on travel logistics and is intended to help you create a framework of preparation for efficient and pleasant travel days.

As a digital nomad, it's important to be strategic about travel and transitions, otherwise the lifestyle can lose its luster.

Define Your Travel Type

Frequency: How Nomadic Are You?

Think about your travel plans holistically - revisit the self-assessment at the start of this book. Are you looking to go to a new location for three to six months? Or are you planning to travel consistently throughout one region, spending a few days or a week a time?

What are your overall goals for your travels and experience abroad? Are you looking for long-term immersive experiences or short stays while acquiring new passport stamps?

Knowing how often you will be traveling is one factor in determining how much time and money you'll invest in the transportation itself.

Location: Research What Matters

Part of the life of a digital nomad is constantly daydreaming and brainstorming the locations you want to explore - we find ourselves caught in a moment debating whether we'd rather spend a few weeks of summer in Prague or Paris, for example. But there are important considerations to keep in mind, most of which we've already covered back in the *Location Scouting* chapter.

Before you book transportation to another country, make sure you've done the appropriate research about any travel restrictions, visas, safety, weather, political climate, and any other potential impediments to travel.

Visas

Research the appropriate visa and how to get it. This, of course, varies for your home country. Check your home country's State Department website for up-to-date requirements as well as the local country's government site to learn about visa application options, if needed.

Many online services advertise that they will handle your visa application for free. Be very hesitant of these services because usually you can easily obtain the visa on your own – in an embassy or consulate, online, or on arrival. Regardless, before making any plans or purchasing any tickets, make sure you can actually travel to your desired country and know how long you can stay!

Pro Tip:

You may be asked for an exit confirmation when going to a new location (check the visa requirements beforehand!). If you don't want to commit to purchasing for a specific day or know your next location, you could use a service, such as FlyOnward.com, that purchases a ticket to anywhere on a date, which you have access to the confirmation materials for 24 or 48 hours. The service then returns the flight, but you keep the confirmation of the rented ticket in your email to show if requested.

Trains, Planes, and Automobiles

The best mode of transportation – how you get from point A to point B – changes based on your location and needs, and you should research the best options for your particular regions and destinations.

For example, Europe has a robust train system, and buses are often not only more affordable but have less strict baggage restrictions. Ferries and boats are also options for slow travel, a sightseeing trip, or perhaps even the only way to reach your next destination.

Peter says:

As an uninformed American, I had previously assumed the best mode of transport was always by air. Recently, I found myself spending a few days in London, and then I was able to hop on a train at King's Cross very easily and arrive in Paris only a few hours later.

Several weeks later, I needed to go from Barcelona to Madrid, but the flight and train tickets were both expensive. However, I was able to travel by bus very cheaply, and when considering transit time to and from the airport plus security and baggage, the total travel time by flight and bus were approximately the same.

Another example is when my friend Evan and I decided to visit Berlin on a weekend, and we were coming from Prague, approximately four hours by train. We purchased tickets - around $50 each - and were shocked when we arrived at the station that not only did we not have assigned seats, but every ticket was standing room only.

During the train ride, we had to make multiple stops, increasing the time, and ultimately it was one of the worst train experiences I've ever had On the way back, we purchased a Flixbus ticket for less than the train ticket, had a reserved and comfortable seat, and made it back in less time.

When planning your travel, consider the cost of your time. If you're billing clients at $100 / hour, then spending 17 hours on a bus without connectivity and ruining yourself for another work day to recover might not really be worth a lower price than investing in the ticket for a 3 hour flight.

In South America, while the continent boasts a well-organized bus transit system between the major cities, the distance and road conditions often equate to lengthy travel times on the ground. For example, traveling by bus from Buenos Aires, it takes about 20 hours to Santiago or 50 hours to La Paz. However, a direct flight is only a few hours.

As a working and traveling professional, your time is money. So to save a hundred (or more) dollars but extend your travel time by hours might end up costing you more productivity in the long run. Especially for those who travel between locations frequently, it may be more important to be efficient in your method of travel than to be cheap.

Another consideration is that, as a nomad, you probably don't *have* to arrive to your next destination in a hurry or on a specific date. You could consider a bus or boat route that takes you to several other off-the-beaten-path destinations along the way. Taking several buses or trains between two major locations can be a viable and interesting option.

Peter says:

Nomad Cruise, a service that runs a cruise ship for digital nomads from South America to Europe (and vice versa) offers an attractive alternative to simply flying between the two continents.

Several members of our Remote Year cohort opted for this method, and while the internet was spotty (at best) in the middle of the Atlantic, there were ample networking opportunities, and they enjoyed taking that route overall.

To Procrastinate or Plan Ahead?

Some digital nomads are planners; they will know exactly where they will be for the next several months, how they will get there, where they will live, and how much it costs - well in advance of actually going. If this is you, then more power to you. There is nothing worse than rushing to make your plane, not remembering if you packed everything. It's even better to be able to give friends and family back home your itinerary - you're more likely to have visitors with detailed plans.

That being said, it's not a requirement. Yes, plane tickets do increase in price at the last minute, but it might be worth it to not be locked into a schedule that might have worked when you booked it, but as the date approaches becomes less ideal.

Meeting new friends may cause you to want to deviate from the plan, new opportunities may arise, or work-related changes may cause you to need to travel to another part of the world or simply stay put for longer. Delaying your purchase of tickets onward could be considered an insurance policy against the cost of itinerary changes.

It's wise to plan ahead and know where you're going and when - but you don't *have* to be a detailed travel planner to succeed as a digital nomad. In fact, the sweet-spot is to have a mix of both personalities.

You should have your broad strokes planned out in advance: the general region you want to see and for how long, what visas you will need to get in advance, etc. However, if you buy a one-way ticket, that gives you freedom to figure out what's next as you gain more information.

Being a nomad is part planning and part serendipitous adventure, which you should embrace as an advantage of the lifestyle.

Ready To Book?

When you are ready to commit to an itinerary, there are some very good sites and apps that help you find the best value when you are attempting to purchase tickets.

- **Rome2Rio:** This website shows the various ways to travel between two or more destinations. For example, if you are trying to visit Paris, Barcelona, Prague, and Belgrade, then the website will show you the best route through those cities as well as the most efficient means of transportation between them, suggesting times and prices for flights, buses, and taxis. While this site is a good starting point, they make money through affiliate programs and selling through specific ticket vendors, so this site should be one of several research sources. Make sure to purchase directly from the airline or bus company. https://www.rome2rio.com/

- **Google Flights:** Google Flights is a very intuitive process, and it's good for estimating prices of flights and easily understanding the most direct routes between locations. They recommend flight options on both major and budget airlines, and then you are directed to book on the airline's site itself. You can also explore a flight map where you choose a starting point or destination, and then it will show prices to/from other cities that fly there. Google is constantly supporting this product, so there is minimal risk of it going away. https://www.google.com/flights/

- **Skyscanner:** SkyScanner provides good prices and alerts, so even though their user interface feels a little crowded and unintuitive, you'll probably find the best prices available. Some smaller airlines that don't appear in most other flight aggregators appear here. https://www.skyscanner.net/
- **Credit Card Portals:** If you have a travel credit card, it likely includes a portal for booking travel (flights, hotels, and rental cars). While it allows you to use points to pay for travel, you can always pay with the credit card itself, and sometimes their results are considerably more affordable than what you'll find elsewhere. It's worth adding to your checklist as one of your research sources.
- **Other:** Kayak, Expedia, Orbitz, Travelocity, and other sites also search flights so you can compare options. At the end of the day, use the service and interface you enjoy and find success with.

(Note: See the *Digital Nomad Tool Kit* for a complete list of recommendations + reference links.)

Travel Tips and Tricks

- **Baggage Fees:** Always pay for your baggage in advance (when booking your flight), and ensure that you know exactly how many kilograms the limit is. Don't wait until check-in at the airport or you will pay much more than you would have hoped, especially on the budget airlines (such as AirAsia and RyanAir). They make plenty of profit from unprepared travellers and overweight luggage. If you are asked to check your carry-on bag at the gate, make sure to grab your laptop and any valuables from your bag. Remember: your hardware is your life, don't let it out of your sight!

- **Cheap Flight Alerts:** It might be prudent to sign up for a service that alerts you when an airline is advertising a flight at a price well below market rate. One example is Scott's Cheap Flight Alerts, which is a service that sends cheap flights to your email whenever the tickets drop below 30-40% cheaper than normal. "Error fares" can be a good way to save, especially if you are not picky about where to go next.
- **Lounge Access:** Depending on how frequently you plan to travel, it may make sense to get a credit card that also comes with worldwide airline lounge access. This feature comes paired with travel-centric credit cards; you'll want to look for cards that offer services such as LoungeClub or PriorityPass. With the credit card, you are also given a membership card that allows you access many different airline lounges across the world.

There is nothing quite like being able to relax with free food and drink during a long layover, as opposed to fighting for outlet space on the outside. Lounges also often have showers (with toiletries and towels) and considerably more comfortable seating options.

Seasoned digital nomads and other globetrotters are already using these travel-friendly cards, and lounges relieve some of the pain of long travel days.

If you don't have a credit card with lounge access, you can either buy a Priority Pass membership on your own, or you can pay the individual lounge fee (it varies, but often is around $25-40, which could be worth the price of food, a quiet space, and a shower).

Some airports also have showers, spas, or gyms (with showers) that you can use for a fee. This may be a cheaper alternative to using a lounge, or help you get a workout or massage in during your layover.

Pro Tip:

Once you've started booking your trip, use apps like Google Trips, Google Calendar, Google Docs, Evernote, TripCase, Pana, etc to record your reservations. Google Calendar will automatically import flight confirmations from emails sent to your Gmail address.

Katherine says:

When I'm booking travel, I immediately copy and paste the reservation code, addresses, amount paid, travel details, and any other pertinent information into a Google calendar event. I schedule it for a few hours before my departure time and set the notification to email me that morning or the night before.

This way, it's all saved in my phone's calendar for offline access, and I have a reminder in the top of my inbox.

I also invite my parents to the event, so they always know when I'm traveling and have the necessary information to find me in case of emergency.

When I'm planning a bigger trip or moving to a new destination, I create a Google doc or Evernote and copy in not only my reservation information but also any local tips for what to eat, things to do, and side trips to take.

Key Takeaways: Travel and Transportation

- The best approach is a combination of "going with the flow" and preparing in advance.

- There are a handful of websites and apps to make price hunting useful - plan out your route and determine what your goals are, and make use of the websites to get the best price.
- Travel days can be stressful, so do what you can ahead of time to minimize cost and discomfort: pre-book baggage, get an airline lounge pass, and load your computer with books or movies.

JOBS & WORKING

"How do digital nomads manage work while traveling?"

AS MUCH AS the *Four Hour Work Week* and other similar motivational nomadic books would have you believe the opposite, the truth is that you will have to work hard (sometimes harder) as a digital nomad, at least initially.

Just as your lifestyle at home would entail commuting, working, and getting paid, life a digital nomad is largely similar, though it has some different challenges and benefits.

Demands on a Digital Nomad

While the commute may be shorter and you likely have fewer coworkers around, nomads still should produce the same amount of work product or deliverables as they would back in an office.

Being a successful digital nomad means keeping a steady source of income, setting and maintaining client expectations, and enjoying professional fulfillment - and it won't come naturally to everyone right away.

Remote workers generally face these challenges that you don't find in typical office jobs:

- **Different Time Zones:** You may find yourself hours or even days behind or ahead of where you are telecommuting to, so working at odd hours can be challenging and tiresome.

- **Communication Frequency**: Being remote means not being able to walk over to coworkers or a boss to ask questions.
- **Office Comforts**: Comfy desk chairs, secondary monitors, and free coffee are some of the perks that don't always exist when you can work from anywhere. Establishing consistent output when you are moving frequently or in a new environment can require determination and self-discipline

Don't worry – while it may sound like a lot of pressure, this chapter focuses on providing you with pointers on how to continue producing good work. These examples of what to do, and what not to do, should help you avoid the mistakes that others have made and set yourself up for success.

Setting Expectations - For Yourself

Think about your professional goals and your expectations around the work you want to do, what you want to achieve professionally, and how you are most productive.

Being a digital nomad is often as much about doing interesting and fulfilling work as it is about exploring new destinations. Despite all the photos you may see to the contrary, successful and long-term nomads work a lot—but perhaps more efficiently.

Outside of your main job or clients, there's usually the freedom to spend time on side projects. The sense of agency over your time and schedule is one of the most fulfilling aspects of the lifestyle.

Many readers of *The 4-hour Work Week* take away that they will work fewer hours, but that isn't the point of Tim Ferris's message. He promotes work efficiency over work quantity – and it's important to keep in mind that establishing the right work-life balance as nomad can be trickier than at home.

With the distractions of travel and meeting new people, as well as being in foreign surroundings, you will likely have less free time (at first) until you develop the habits and self-discipline to make remote working in a foreign country possible.

The key, however, is to work smarter, and eventually you won't have to work harder. So if your goal is to travel as much as possible while maintaining a job, then getting the most output per hour of work is what you'll want to strive for on a daily basis.

One of the most important things you will need to do is set yourself up with clear routines. Tim Chimoy is a digital nomad architect and entrepreneur who is based between Berlin and Bangkok throughout the year. He writes on his blog about the importance of the routines:

> *Many [digital nomads] want to escape the routines and thus find the location independent life so fascinating. That's how I felt too. Routines quickly become boring for me. I always have to break out of them.*
>
> *But the truth is: As crazy it may sound, it is essential to create routines within the lack of structure.*

> TIM CHIMOY

Tim's point is a realistic insight of how to create a sustainable location-independent life. Routines are the basis of a digital nomad catch 22:

> *In order to escape the routine of our 9-to-5 jobs and life back home, we decide to travel abroad. But to make that lifestyle*

work successfully, we need to establish even more rigorous routines on the road.

Develop a schedule for yourself and test it out for a few weeks at a time - and obviously your travel schedule will impact what's feasible. This is one reason why spending more time per place may be a more sustainable approach to travel, or at least a good way to start.

As you move to various time zones and locations, your routine may need to adapt. If you can keep a journal and track your time, productivity, sleep, and overall feelings of happiness or restedness, you can discover what habits and routines work best for you.

Setting Expectations - For Your Clients

You will inevitably have to prove that you can be a quality remote worker, so that your clients, managers, and customers realize they can still rely on you to manage your responsibilities even though you're far away. If you work with new clients consistently, you may have to do this on a pretty regular interval.

You may not have clients per se; it could be a manager at the headquarters back home, a business partner that depends on you, customers that purchase your products online, or perhaps it's your coworkers, suppliers, and investors that need to be considered. Basically, anyone that depends on you is someone who needs to see that your lifestyle is not only non-disruptive but productive.

There are a couple key points you will need to demonstrate:

- You can work around their schedule, and you can be available on regular hours so that it doesn't feel like you've gone off the map.

- Your communication is consistent, and both your clients and teammates feel connected to you.
- You can still deliver as quality of output as before (or even better, hopefully!)
- You aren't just sipping tropical drinks at the beach while they're working.

Additionally, it's important to start by asking what metrics they're most concerned about and ensure you address those upfront and on a regular basis.

If you start working with someone new, it's important to demonstrate your reliability early by establishing a workflow right away. It's important to set boundaries to avoid being overworked, while staying flexible and sensitive to their needs and concerns.

If you're newly transitioning into remote work, outline your various tasks, roles, deliverables, meetings, and relationships. Write out how you currently manage them and how that will change (or not) when you go remote.

Defining, explaining, and planning everything in writing will not only assuage their fears but will help clarify what you need to manage.

Pro Tips: Managing your clients remotely

- **Establish Office Hours:** Especially in the tech industry, communication is established via instant message, and response time is generally expected to be relatively short. However, across time zones, this is often is a challenge. What you should do is communicate when you can be expected to be at the computer and ready to reply. Make sure everyone you work with knows these: put your timezone in your email signature, and make sure to highlight to your clients or boss whenever you switch zones. As long as you're consistent, people will accept your work hours.

- **Your Daily Work Schedule:** If you are in Asia and need to work USA hours, you will likely need to decide whether you are going to be working late or waking up early, as 9 am PST is midnight in most of Asia. You may find mornings are easier, letting you work and still enjoy a good amount of daytime to explore. Others prefer splitting work between daytime and late nights, so they have daylight hours and early evening available for themselves. When you're working, think in terms of the time zone you are working in tandem with. That way, you will be less likely to miss any meetings or deadlines. If you are sending emails during what would be sleeping hours for the recipient, you can install Boomerang for your email client, so you can schedule emails to be sent during their working hours.

- **Frequent Communication:** This goes for almost all remote work, but peers and stakeholders both like to hear progress and get nervous when someone goes dark for a while, even if they are still working hard. As much as it can seem trivial, making sure clients are happy is often as easy as letting them know you're there. Even "no update today" is still an update, and go a long way at staving off potential crisis. Creating a calendar reminder for daily check-ins can be smart, depending on relationship with the particular client or boss.

While setting up a company or team workflow to facilitate remote work requires additional upfront work and revising processes, it also results in a more consciously designed system, with employees who are both more communicative and proactive in their roles.

For example, when I was the remote Head of Production for a design studio, the creative director and I learned to communicate through a variety of new technology and apps— Slack, Basecamp, Asana, Google apps, Evernote, Box, Dropbox, Zoom — that make it easy for us to work together regardless of physical location or proximity.

Ultimately, an employee that is able to work remotely proves that they're really capable, good at time management and invested in their job and company. Remote work is a great litmus test for employee performance: the company will either replace a less competent or uninterested employee that fails to make it work, or they make a great team member happier and more successful.

Whether an employee wants to try short-term options or attempt a formal program like Remote Year, remote work can facilitate access to a varied network, new sources of inspiration and a shift in work-life balance that can be tremendously beneficial — not only for the individual, but their teams, clients and employer, too. - Katherine

While your personal professional development may not be at the forefront of their minds, it can be something to discuss and use to sell the benefit of your new lifestyle. Can your travels bring you to meetings with clients abroad? Can you find networking opportunities to meet other professionals in your field and learn more about innovations and best practice?

One benefit of being a digital nomad is that you can meet people from all walks of life, industries, and roles, either through socializing, networking events, or working side-by-side in a cafe or coworking space. How can that benefit translate into something for your client or company?

Where to Work Work Work Work Work

You should be able to work from your primary accommodation, as a general guideline, but if you are in a location for longer than a few days, it makes sense to branch out a bit and work either at cafes or coworking spaces. Remote Year, for example, provides participants with a membership at a local coworking space.

Coworking spaces are often some of the best places to work as they typically provide 24/7 access, high speed internet, and light refreshments. They also often host networking, professional development, and social events, so you can more easily meet locals, expats, and other digital nomads. After you do your research, ask for a tour when you arrive, and test it out with a day pass to see if it's a good match for you.

What makes a good co-working space?

Good internet, access to private call rooms, air conditioning, and a good sense of community.

The other option is cafes, but their receptiveness to nomads varies by location. When you find a place that suits your needs, make sure to keep your footprint small and purchase items regularly to justify using their space and wifi. Nomads who go to cafes and talk loudly on Skype, occupy a seat for hours on end, and don't purchase much make us all look bad.

For example, in Chiang Mai, the Nimman Square cafes (the area with the highest concentration of digital nomads and expats) have figured out how to police this behavior. The CAMP cafe and work place has a 2 hour wifi code for each 50 baht spent on drinks, and, next door, the Tom N Tom Cafe has table minimums: 200 baht on food and drinks for a small table or 300 baht for a table by the window.

There are several websites with a directory of coworking spaces and digital nomad friendly cafes, including:

- Copass — A global membership that lets you access a network of independent coworking spaces, fablabs, hacker spaces or any type of collaborative spaces and people with one single account.
- Workfrom — The best places in a city to work remotely, based on recommendations by actual remote workers. See WiFi speeds, plugs, food and more before you go.
- Coworking Map — Our goal is to map all the spaces on the planet, marking its location by anyone!
- RemoteSeats — We take beautiful unused restaurant spaces and make them available to a community of business travelers, creatives, and entrepreneurs.

Productivity Hacks

Working remotely can be awesome because you can often find yourself working at peak efficiency thanks to stripping away time-wasters found in typical office jobs: client meetings, internal meetings, morning meetings, all-hands meetings… you get the picture.

But to achieve the glorious state of maximum productivity requires fairly strict self-discipline. Here are some helpful hacks digital nomads have reported that work for them:

- **Pomodoro Technique**: A productivity management tool so powerful, it even has its own Wikipedia page. The technique entails using a pattern of working and breaks until a set task is completed. A person will work for 25 minutes straight, ignoring and writing down any distractions, and then taking a 5 minute break after the 25 minutes to address the interrupting tasks. After a set of 4 of these, the person will then take a longer 15-30 minute break. This technique is a tool that helps people break larger projects into manageable chunks. **Pro Tip:** Search the App Store for timers that help you do this – Tomato Timer and Forest are some apps with this functionality.

- **Cloud-Based To Do Lists**: Try to get integrated with a software solution that helps manage your to-do list and daily action items, and make liberal use of it. Even better, find a solution that is cross-platform, so your to-dos can be accessed on your desktop, as well as your phone or tablet, so it can become a regular routine. Write everything down, even small tasks you are sure to get done, which helps reinforce positive feelings of completeness by checking off items regularly. Smaller, bite-sized pieces can be easier to tackle than one large project. You can play around with many free services to help with this, such as Evernote, Any Do, Wunderlist, Trello, or even Google Sheets.

- **Nice Hotels and Bars:** If you ever find yourself out and about but with little time until you need to be online for some reason, look on Google Maps for the typical 4 or 5 star hotel names (Hilton, Four Seasons, Hyatt, etc) because you can almost always guarantee they will have fast and reliable internet that you can access easily. Just sit in the lobby or bar area, order something to eat or drink (or even just look like you are waiting for someone or are staying in the hotel), and you'll likely be able to take care of your business for a couple hours.

Collaboration and Networking

In general, most digital nomads embrace the entrepreneurial spirit, and we thrive on collaboration with one another, sharing ideas over coffee, or listening to each other present their current ventures. It's also important to stay in touch with like-minded folks to brainstorm, discuss, and even start projects while on the road.

This book is a good example of something that can be accomplished by working together, as Peter and Katherine set out to write and publish this book after meeting on Remote Year and then traveling separately for several months.

The Remote Year program aims to foster creativity and professional development, and they help organize a monthly networking event called "The Junction," where RY participants and local business owners and entrepreneurs come together for a few presentations and casual conversation. Speakers have ranged from local artists to consultants and non-profits to investors, and venues have been coworking spaces, upscale restaurants, cocktail bars, and company headquarters.

Hacker Paradise also runs collaboration focused programming with regular networking events. Members of HP have met with local entrepreneurs in Japan and attended skills workshops in Portugal. Demo days were weekly events, which helped incentivize producing quality work.

One nomad we interviewed, who spent time with both Remote Year and Hacker Paradise, found Hacker Paradise a bit more "work-focused" while Remote Year was more "community-centric."

Joining a coworking space may help you get involved with networking and development events within the local community. Additionally, if you are in a larger city, check MeetUp groups for professionally oriented topics as well as CouchSurfing activities.

LinkedIn and Google searches can also yield interesting contacts, and people in foreign countries are often receptive to people reaching out to express an interest in meeting, particularly startup founders and other expats.

Now that the digital nomad movement is growing, there are more events at coworking spaces, in digital nomad "hubs," and featuring remote workers + travelers. In February 2017, Katherine and a few friends attended a Digital Nomad Summit in Chiang Mai, which had 350+ attendees and 9 speakers on topics ranging from UX design, marketing online courses, and design hacks to self-care and purpose.

Case Study: Nomad Collaboration In Action

Although Adelaida and her business partner Jeff were both participants in Remote Year, they were on separate programs (different groups run by Remote Year). They only met each other when Adelaida went home to Bogota where coincidentally Jeff was taking some time to explore the area as well. They connected through their RY affiliation.

Fed up with the challenges of keeping up with friends and meeting interesting people who are also traveling, they put their heads together to create a service that help you stay in touch with wherever your friends are in the world, where they are planning on visiting next, and provides a platform for planning trips together so you don't lose touch.

Their service is called Nomo Fomo, a play on words for "no more fear of missing out."

Ultimately Nomo Fomo was built to solve a problem that has been around for ages and continues to grow. As technology allows us to move further away from our family and friends as well as connect with people all over the world, it is hard to connect with people outside of the digital world.

We realized that the more we travel, the harder it is to decide where to go as well as who to invite. Even though we may want to invite all of our friends to our frequently created trips, we feel like there isn't a social platform out there to blast it out to everyone without looking like you're showing off or rubbing it in.

ADELAIDA DIAZ-ROA

They believe that their service will help facilitate longer term friendships and ultimately further empower the digital nomad lifestyle because it will help people stay in touch with those they meet on their travels through foreign countries.

Nomo Fomo will give digital nomads an ability to help connect with each other at any point and in many ways. This will allow them to join their friends on their next adventure; whether it be a new city to live in or a hike up Mount Kilimanjaro.

You also run into the problem of your paths crossing with friends but somehow still missing them because you are usually reactive (seeing a post about a trip on Facebook or hearing through the grapevine) versus proactive (reaching out to a friend to see when they will be in a city you plan to visit next month).

We built Nomo Fomo around the idea that, by allowing you to connect with all of your friends and share your travel details, you can find new places to meet up as well as the ability to never have a "missed connection" when you are in the same city or event as someone you know.

JEFF WALSH

Their product is in beta right now, and they hope to launch sometime in 2017. You can keep up with their progress on their page: Facebook.com/NomoTravelFomo.

Key Takeaways: Jobs and Working

- You'll end up working harder at first to establish your remote working lifestyle. Make sure to set boundaries while also remaining flexible on the work hours.
- Get yourself comfortable using various pieces or cloud-based productivity tools to help make life easier.
- Take ownership of your professional career by integrating with the local coworking spaces, entrepreneurship groups, or simply meet-up and network with people working on interesting projects.

TECHNOLOGY

"What are the best devices to use as a digital nomad?"

AS A DIGITAL NOMAD, you'll come to realize that your new mantra is "home is where there's wifi." You'll rely heavily on your devices and technology in tandem with a halfway-decent internet connection to get your work done and maintain this lifestyle.

Travel Smart(Phone)

The first key piece of technology is your phone. It will be one of the most precious and valuable tools you'll have: it is your light when you can't see (literally), your guide when you are lost, your local expert when you have a question, and your gateway to making new friends on the fly. It also will be your primary source of capturing memories and keeping in touch with friends, family, and work.

The actual type of phone is a matter of personal preference. We don't recommend getting a brand new phone for the road, however. A new phone is more of a liability than a luxury in this lifestyle - phones are the most common casualties of travel, whether they've been stolen, misplaced, or broken.

Your choice of phone should be one that you feel comfortable maneuvering around quickly at night, and one that you won't be heartbroken if it ended up missing. Of course it needs to run the necessary applications, have sufficient memory, and take quality photos, too.

General Phone Requirements:

- **Tethering**: It needs to be able to function as a mobile hotspot using your SIM card data when wifi is not readily available. This is a crucial lifehack for digital nomads, as you may find yourself in the middle of nowhere (or just unlucky with the internet) and have an important client call coming up in a few minutes.

- **Ample Storage**: You'll inevitably take countless photos of your journeys and everyday life on the road, so 32 GB of storage is a recommended minimum. You should also consider paying for a subscription storage service such as iCloud, Google Drive, or Dropbox to automatically sync your precious photographs to ensure that in the case of a phone being lost or stolen, your pictures are safe in the cloud. Hardware can be replaced, but photos can't.

- **Accessories:** A separate battery pack to charge your phone will be a life-saver whether you aren't always able to get to an outlet or you're using the phone more than average for work or navigation. At least 10,000 mAH capacity should provide more than a single phone recharge. A sturdy case as well as a tempered glass screen protector are both beneficial in preventing damage from the inevitable drops and scratches. While it's not a necessity, a portable speaker is often a great accessory for casual social gatherings, road trips, and outdoor activities.

Prevention is your best method to prolonging the life of your phone and avoiding expensive replacement fees. Even with warranty and insurance plans, you would could find yourself thousands of miles away from the nearest Apple Store, facing heavy customs fees for shipping a new one, or paying expensive prices for imported devices.

Data: Staying Online Around The World

There are two main approaches of mobile data solutions on the road: subscribing to an international plan and using local SIMs. Wifi-only is an option, but it's less advisable for long-term travel.

Regardless, it's better to use few international calls or texts, and instead prioritize data for communicating with others. This means you're looking for data plans for 2G, 3G or LTE networks, not minutes or SMS. With data, you can use services that rely on internet (like messaging apps).

International Plans

There are several companies that offer international plans for customers. The upsides are that you will not need to consistently research, track down, and purchase a new SIM card in each country you visit. You should consider this option if you are planning to take many side trips or regularly switch your location. The downsides are that these plans can be a bit pricey, and often roaming data speeds are capped.

Peter says:

I am currently subscribed to T-Mobile "Simple Choice" plan, which gives 10GB unlimited 2G data speeds in 130+ countries. While data speeds and price can be better with local SIMs, I travel to new countries on a regular basis, and the ease of having the phone work as soon as I arrive is important to me. If you are staying places for longer periods of time, it might not be the best solution for you.

Some people also use Project Fi, a service from Google, as an affordable solution that works worldwide. Project Fi "automatically connects you to the best available signal, whether that's Wi-Fi or one of our three 4G LTE partner networks."

Local SIM Plans

In almost every country, you can find a telecom kiosk either at the airport, sold at the counter in corner stores, or at booths around the typical tourist spots. You purchase a SIM card that you can put into your phone that will give you data for between 7 and 30 days, usually at the highest speed the country can support. Depending on the country, this can also be relatively inexpensive – airport SIM cards are typically more expensive than ones purchased in-town.

Peter says:

In Belgrade, Serbia, I paid around $3 for a week's worth of unlimited LTE data. However, in the Amsterdam airport, the price was $40 for 1 GB of data.

It's a good idea to research the best companies, plans, and prices before arrival in a new area. With this approach, you will get highest data speeds and can often spend less money. However, you will have to weigh this against managing data limits and durations, as well as locating a store regularly while traveling.

There is a helpful Wiki site that helps people learn about data packages and pricing across the world, which we have linked to on this book's website.

The Wifi-Only Plan

Some folks decide to rely on finding wifi to operate their phones. This could be free public wifi found in some cities - Barcelona and Buenos Aires, for example - or from coffee shops, restaurants, and your accommodations.

We do not recommend this as your only source of access for your phone, both for the sake of safety and prioritizing your professional needs. Even if you are on a tight budget, it is still important to be able to reach out in case of emergencies. Instagramming on the go might be a luxury, but finding your way back home safely is a necessity.

Pro Tip:

Be mindful of data caps and apps that might use a lot of data. Snapchat and Instagram are examples of big data users, as sending videos requires significant data.

In your phone's settings, you can turn off cellular data for individual apps, which means you can't use them until you're connected to wifi. Managing your cellular data settings for most apps will save you data and money as well as help extend your phone's battery life.

There's An App for That

These are just a handful of the apps you might find helpful as a digital nomad, whether you're communicating with friends and family, navigating your way around a new city, looking for dates, or adjusting to a different location.

Whatsapp

Everyone in the world (outside of the USA) uses Whatsapp as the primary means of communicating. It's not the prettiest or most feature-rich chat app on the market, but it allows for individual and group chats with the ability to send location pins, voice memos, images, and links. Some data packages do not count Whatsapp use against the limit as well, which is a nice bonus.

You should be aware that Whatsapp uses the original number you sign up as the authentication, so as you switch SIM cards and get new numbers, you want to tell Whatsapp to keep your original number. In many Asian countries, Line is the dominant app, but generally people there use Whatsapp as well.

Google Maps

The go-to maps application. For iOS users, the built-in maps app is not very good, especially abroad. A particularly useful feature is the ability to download offline maps for most cities. Doing this prior to arrival means you can access the local map area offline, so you can quickly and reliably navigate prior to getting your SIM card or when you might not have the best internet connection. Keep your wifi setting on, though, so that it pings around to locate your blue dot on the map.

Instagram

Some people find that posting constantly to Facebook with updates of your travels to be a bit boastful. Instagram is a better way to catalog your travels while also allowing your friends and family to decide if they want to get updates or not.

Additionally, Instagram has a location-based map feature that tags your uploads to locations, creating an interesting timeline of your travels. It can also be a helpful research and networking tool as most digital nomads use Instagram, and looking up hotels, cafes, and venues (by location or hashtag) shows recent and popular images taken by real people.

Tinder

Tinder can be one of the most surprisingly useful apps while traveling. Tinder is a location-based app, largely used for dating (although not exclusively), where users decide if they are interested in a person (by swiping their picture right) or if they do not (by swiping left). The app (rightfully) has a reputation as a "hookup tool," and if that is your end-goal, you might find success. Beyond that, you can use it as a way to meet a local or other traveler, who could show you around their home town or explore with you.

The user base is surprisingly global, with users in all major cities. With the premium subscription, you can match and chat with users in a location before you even arrive. This can be useful to get tips on places to go and set up plans in advance. It's a worthwhile addition to your app list if meeting people is a priority to you.

EveryTimeZone.com

This helps localize your life. When you first make it to Asia, it can be very hard to wrap your head around what the timezone is for your clients. Most likely, you will need to be able to available during their business hours in the Americas or Europe, and missing a meeting can damage client confidence in your lifestyle.

XE Currency

A currency app is important to have on hand as you adjust to new conversation rates and can help you stick to your budget more effectively.

Your Most Prized Possession

Obviously, in order to travel, live, and work remotely via the internet, you need to have a reliable and appropriate computer to successfully maintain your job and income. You may travel with your current laptop, but consider your needs carefully. If you have an older laptop now, it may be worth buying a new one before starting your trip.

What you need depends primarily on what you do for work. Do you run heavy software like Adobe Photoshop or Final Cut Pro? In that case, you'll need to bring a powerful machine, such as a Macbook Pro or Microsoft Surface Book.

If you aren't required to run some process intensive software, you may want to consider to a lighter, more portable machine, especially if most of your work is browser-based (aka email and internet usage instead of running apps / programs).

A Chromebook is a computer series that runs the operating system ChromeOS. You can do all of the same things as if you were using the Chrome browser on another computer. They are incredibly light and portable, have phenomenal battery life, and are very affordably priced. The downside is that you can only do things in the Chrome browser. So if 90% of your job is email, then this is a machine that might be a good match as it easy to travel with and is not as big of a loss if it does get damaged.

The Microsoft Surface and the Macbook Air are the most popular laptops for digital nomads. If you do not need to have an expensive laptop, you should not bring one. Take what you need to get your work done effectively, and no more. A lighter and smaller laptop means less weight, a smaller bag (or more stuff in a big bag), and will save your back when you are walking around town.

Pro Tip: Laptop Accessory Suggestions

- Backup laptop charger
- Portable power adapter, with a current converter attached and USB outlets for phone charging
- Hardshell protective case and a soft sleeve for carrying / storage
- If you need a mouse, try to find one that is bluetooth and that charges via USB

Regardless of which computer you pick, you need to protect it. Use a hard-shell protector for the outside and have a padded, potentially waterproof carrying case for transporting it in your bag, purse, or backpack. As with the phones, having insurance or a warranty plan is great, though location, customs, and local prices make any repair or replacement a prohibitive experience.

Staying Safe and Sound

The key is making the lifestyle as sustainable as possible. Your whole job is working out of a laptop, and you risk a lot if something happens to it.

Kipp, a digital nomad from New York, was traveling through South America when he had many of his electronics stolen out of his hotel room in Cusco, Peru: "They took everything: my computer, camera, animation equipment... even my passport."

The security footage showed that a man entered the hotel and had a key to his room - potentially because someone knew that there were thousands of dollars worth of electronics inside. However, a potential travesty was downgraded to an inconvenience, thanks to travel insurance. Within days, his claim was processed and he was able to purchase new devices. "I still had to go back to New York to renew my passport," he lamented. "But the insurance on my stuff saved me."

Research a solid insurance plan for your phone and computer, potentially through your or your family's homeowners insurance, a travel insurance plan, or a specific traveler's technology insurance plan.

Jono Lee, a product designer, wrote an extensive piece about securing your digital life while on the road. Here are a few of his suggestions, though it's well worth the read and research as he gives specific advice, reasoning, and recommendations.

- *Every account should have a unique password, and they should be complex*
- *Use 2 factor authentication (2FA)*
- *Set alerts so you can immediately address suspicious activity*
- *Use a Virtual Private Network (VPN)*
- *Use the HTTPS Everywhere browser extension*
- *Set a password on your smartphone or laptop*
- *Use a USB condom (protect against data theft at USB charging stations)*
- *Use RFID blocking sleeves (for credit cards, passport, etc)*
- *Use a webcam cover*

- *MacBooks haven't had a lock bracket area since the generation before the Retina MacBook Pro, but thankfully there are brackets you can add on.*
- *Enable your device's built in tracking software, which all major platforms have today.*
- *Keep important files in the cloud & back up your laptop to an external hard drive regularly*
- *Research device, travel property, and homeowners insurance options*

JONO LEE

Jono specifically lists several insurance options: AppleCare, Esuranty, and Clements Worldwide International Property Insurance, among some other insurance notes.

Technology Tip: Minimalism and Efficiency

One sacrifice with this lifestyle is the creature comfort of having a home or corporate office. You won't have the ergonomic chair, the second display, the mechanical keyboard, or the Bose headphones.

But it can be a liberating experience. What do you really need to survive? Do you really need to have all the accessories, or can you be equally as productive with less?

Bringing a portable external / secondary monitor is not advisable. This is another expensive piece of equipment that you have to tote from place to place, and you really don't want to be "that guy" who sets up at a coffee shop with an entire Radio Shack display on their table.

Several nomads on Remote Year brought second screens, and everyone who did ended up shipping it back home or trying to sell it before the end of 6 months.

Expensive headphones are targets for theft and take up more space. A small, earbud pair of headphones are the most portable and, coupled with the microphone on the cord, can be sufficient for Skype calls as well.

Our Tried & True Tech

Peter's Inventory

- **Phone**: iPhone 6+ with protective case and tempered glass screen protector.
- **Computer**: Macbook Pro Retina from 2012, covered with hard plastic shell.
- **Tablet**: Samsung Galaxy Tab 2, although if he didn't need it for work, he would have left at home or sold.
- **Accessories**: He always has his Nomad wallet which includes a 2400 mAh battery built in; useful for emergency situations where you have run out of battery in your phone. A wall charger with 4 USB inputs helps charge his devices, and he has a case or shell for everything that he needs to do work from.

Pro Tip: VPN

Consider getting a subscription for a virtual private network. Why? A VPN allows you to encrypt and secure data when working in public spaces as well as visit sites on the internet as if you were located in a different country. It can help when websites give you different information or prices based on your location.

Katherine's Inventory

- **Phone:** iPhone 5 with a Tech21 case (and a backup iPhone 6 with a Tech21 case)
- **Computer:** MacBook 13" Air (refurbished 2013, bought in 2014; 4 GB memory, 250 GB flash storage); Moshi keyguard cover
- **Accessories:** Apple travel adaptor kit, Wacom Intuos Pen & Touch Tablet, Blue Snowball Microphone, Amazon Kindle, SeaGate Slim external hard drive (for laptop Time Machine backups), auto-sync all laptop files to Dropbox

Katherine says:

I've loved my MacBook Air, and getting a refurb from the Apple store got me better memory and longer AppleCare coverage. Having the key cover has protected my computer against drips and dirt, which makes me much more comfortable using it at cafes.

Plus, I keep all my files synced to my Dropbox account, so everything is safe on on the cloud.

I like that the iPhone 5 is smaller and was a hand-me-down, so I've been less stressed about having a really nice phone while traveling. It also fits in my zip wallet and hand easily, which keeps it more secure.

Key Takeaways: Technology

- Your technology is very important - make sure to keep it protected with insurance, cases, and general precautions because a hardware failure could be devastating and expensive.

- Be as productive as possible with the fewest number of devices and avoid redundancy. Unless you really need a tablet or travel monitor, don't bring one!
- Backups on Backups: A backup phone, an external hard drive, and Dropbox or Google cloud services will help you out when you least expect it.

PACKING & POSSESSIONS

"What do I need to pack and bring with me?"

THE ADAGE about tasks taking the amount of time you have available to work on it applies to stuff as well: If you have space to fill, you will fill it. So let's first define what kind of space you will be traveling with as a digital nomad.

What to Lug(gage) Around The World?

Luggage and what you put in it is a bit of a chicken-and-egg situation, but thinking through these questions and deciding on what you want to travel with in terms of luggage can help guide the packing process.

First, you should consider where you will be going, how you will be getting there, and how long you'll be staying in each place. If you're constantly on the move, repacking will lose its charm quickly (if it ever had any), so you'll likely want to have less baggage and less stuff in it.

However, if you plan on being more of a slo-mad and will stay months at a time in each place, perhaps it won't bother you and having to pack and move a large suitcase won't be an issue.

When it comes to cost, most buses don't have a baggage limit (or allow 2 checked bags). Major international flights typically allow 2 bags free. However, domestic/national flights and cheaper airlines may limit to 1 bag and/or 23 kg. Extra baggage fees are often more expensive abroad than on US airlines, so it's important to research your travel methods and the base requirements and excess fees.

For carry-on luggage, some international flights actually have smaller dimensions allowable so be sure to double check your carrier's specific requirements, but standard is usually 22 in x 18 in x 10 in (or 56 cm x 45 cm x 25 cm). Sometimes cabin luggage is limited to 7-10 kg total, so that's another consideration though it's less often checked by airlines if the bag is the appropriate size and can easily be carried by the passenger.

Nomads often downsize the longer they are on the road, regardless of how and where they travel. If you're constantly accumulating more stuff, you can buy new luggage on the road - most major cities have malls with many options available. Whether you're buying a new bag or getting rid of one, visitors from home are often a good way to get exactly what you want or send something home that you aren't necessarily ready to give away.

> Katherine says:
>
> *When I traveled through India and SE Asia for 4 months, I had a large 65-liter backpack plus a purse/laptop bag. Although it was handy to be able to carry everything on my back, it ultimately wasn't an important feature most of the time given how I was traveling.*
>
> *When I came on Remote Year, I decided I wanted enough clothing options for various settings & climates (professional, casual, workouts, cold hikes, beach) and more of my personal comforts (yoga mat, microphone, tablet).*
>
> *I brought a big roller suitcase (with a duffle packed in that sometimes I check as a second bag), a small carry-on suitcase (for electronics, papers, meds, and emergency outfits for lost baggage), and my laptop bag/purse.*

When it comes to what specific articles of luggage to purchase, brand loyalty can play as big of a factor as specifications and cost (and aesthetics). Hard luggage is more durable but heavier and potentially more difficult to manage in some settings. Soft luggage is lightweight and easy to pack but risks damage more easily. Rolling luggage means less carrying but typically also limits mobility.

Many digital nomads opt for a soft-sided rolling suitcase that allows for some flexibility in size and shape while preserving the ease of rolling. Some brands make rolling bags that have a backpack built in – likely not as comfortable as a true backpack for a long travel day but valuable in certain transition settings.

Another important consideration is whether you'll always travel with all your belongings or if you'll make a home base for a month or more and then take "side trips." In that case, having a large bag that travels only for major transitions plus a small weekend trip duffle or backpack might make the most sense.

One approach might be thinking through your packing list, assembling everything you'll want long-term, and measuring the dimensions / volume that requires, as well as what a weekend trip volume would look like. Or borrow someone else's luggage and do a test pack to see how your belongings fit and what might not make the cut (or if you need to expand your size expectations). Then use that in your research of what luggage will fit your lifestyle and packing list.

As with everything, you have to find what fits for you - and know that it might change once you're actually on the road and learning what lifestyle you want to live.

Traveler's Tetris: What Will Fit?

While it's important to carefully think through what you want and need and commit to bringing your best guess at the right things for your long-term lifestyle, don't let the task overwhelm you.

Know that you can always send things home or buy what you need locally, and that many clothing items get worn-to-pieces so you'll do more cycling through clothes than having an extensive, static closet, so to speak.

Think about where you'll be going and when:

- Will your travels consistently be in the same climate?
- If you'll consistently be in warm weather, you'll likely be packing lighter clothes and shoes.
- Colder weather or varying climates means you'll likely need some bulky items and will need clothes that work well in both settings when paired with the right layers.
- What time of year will you be there - is it during a rainy season? Is there a chance of early / late snow or sun?

Then you'll need to consider what you'll be doing:

- Will you spend all your time in casual environments, or will you want nice clothes for professional networking events, client meetings, expensive dinners, and performances?
- What activities will you be doing outside of work and daily life: running / workouts, yoga, swimming, hiking, etc.
- Are you traveling to parts of the world that have cultural considerations for what is appropriate to wear? Even though travel is more common and many people wear whatever they want anywhere, it's better to be a thoughtful traveler and respect local customs to cover arms, legs, head, etc. There may be places - from temples to nightclubs - that will not allow you to enter with knees, shoulders, and/or head uncovered, so be sure you have options available.

Of course, there are endless personal preferences and needs that you'll have to consider and determine, including:

- Medicine and medical devices (and make sure you always pack them in your carry-on luggage)
- Toiletries - shampoo, lotion, makeup, tampons, razors, etc (but don't forget most things are now available everywhere, though maybe not your favorite brand)

Unzipping A Digital Nomad's Bag

We've collected some packing lists and words of advice from digital nomads. Remote Year participants have documented their strategies and favorite items on many blogs. The program's itinerary means RY nomads can provide a helpful case study of what to bring (or not) for long-term travel through various climates and destination types.

Tiago Almeida originally came on Remote Year with everything in one bag. His approach:

> *Traveling light means not packing many of the "just in case" clothes and gadgets you want. It's thinking about what you can cut instead of what you can add. Going to cold places? Instead of bringing a lot of long coats or hoodies, think about layers.*

TIAGO ALMEIDA

Tiago bought a drone a couple months into Remote Year, which he uses for getting incredible footage of his travels. He's updated his original post and packing list with a summary of what worked, what lasted, and what didn't.

Jessie Lang catalogued her gear and clothes before coming on Remote Year and then updated it at the end, adding reviews of what worked and what didn't: The Ultimate Guide to Packing for a Year.

Write down your travel goals – Are you planning on moving locations every few days or staying put for a few weeks at a time? Will you be in major cities with clean water and sidewalks for suitcases or will you be in more rural and exotic terrain? Does fashion matter or can you get away with wearing the same 3 shirts all the time?

Consider your budget – travel gear can get really expensive if you let it, but it does not have to be. Consider buying second hand through Craigslist or Goodwill. Opt for an "off" brand that provides a quality product but isn't as expensive.

Just do it! – If you have dreams of traveling, don't get caught up in "the perfect packing list" because you'll never find it. Instead, focus on things that work for your purposes right now and don't stress over the rest. The world is a lot more familiar than you may imagine and you can get new clothes or travel gear anywhere you go, often for cheaper!

JESSIE LANG

Arestia Rosenberg recommends keeping life easy by bringing matching items and layers. Her post also includes links to her specific shopping suggestions.

Layers are going to be your best friend, and I'd say 10 days to two weeks worth of outfits is good to rotate through. Stuff you can wear anywhere (cotton dresses that can be dressed up, a pair of black pants for business or going out affairs) is the best way to go, but you know what you wear.

I live in jeans and tank tops and tend to dress those up or down depending. But make sure you take one sexy dress (or

26

one dope jacket if you're a dude). Trust me, you'll wear it at some point.

I am currently traveling with a massive rolling duffel bag from LL Bean and a Kelty 40L backpack (the biggest you can have while carrying on). The backpack is a faithful one and works great for me because it doubles nicely as a side trip bag that I've gone as long as two weeks with stuff in it. I pack a daypack and laptop bag for everyday use once I've settled somewhere in the duffel.

Travel towels, pouches, a collapsible tupperware to make lunches in, even the perfect journal (just write a line a day!).

ARESTIA ROSENBERG

Katherine's Remote Year Packing List

Remote Year meant packing for a full year of my life, and I enjoyed having variety of my belongings with me (especially after 2 years on the road already). Yes, this is my caveat that mine is not a 'pack light, have less!' list.

I've been embarrassed about how much stuff I've had at times, but now it was actually easy enough for me to manage all year. I only paid about $150–200 total in baggage fees, which was reasonable for me for the benefit of having everything I wanted.

But that's just me. Do what works for you. Definitely, pack as little as possible to have what you really want and need.

Our RY2 itinerary ranged from cold + rainy + mountain climates to hot + tropical + beach, so it was good to have a range of options, from semi-formal to workout to hiking to beach clothes, plus gear.

I looked back through my photos of packing days to see what has actually made it around the world with me, from Texas to Montevideo, through South America to Europe to SE Asia.

Here's a top-level summary of what I've had in my bag (and how it fared) throughout my Remote Year:

- *luggage: Eagle Creek rolling suitcase + Herschel duffle + Delsey carry-on rolling suitcase + Lo & Sons OMG bag*
- *extra bags: Herschel packable backpack + Longchamp Le Pliage large + Dakine fanny pack*
- *4 packing cubes — not necessary, but does help me pack in an organized fashion; also protect my clothes from less clean drawers*
- *7+ dresses — a whole outfit in one!*
- *black jeans + nice pants + stretch pants*
- *15+ tops — definitely could cut down*
- *5 x spandex pants — wear them all the time: yoga, running, pajamas, travel day...*
- *4 x workout tanks*
- *merino wool long sleeve top — great in South America as a cold layer*
- *jean jacket + lightweight coat + rain jacket*
- *a million pairs of underwear and socks — I love not having to panic over laundry*
- *2 x bathing suits*
- *2+ scarves — fashion accessory, makeshift pillow, and warm layer*
- *robe — lightweight and comfortable, great for RY hangouts in apartments*
- *Yogo travel yoga mat + Manduka mat towel — love them*

- *emergency medical first aid kit — never opened but seems logical to have*
- *silk pillowcase & an allergy pillow cover — definitely useful in South America*

(Note: Check out the *Digital Nomad Tool Kit* for a simplified general packing checklist.)

Key Takeaways: Packing and Possessions

- Consider your destinations, climate, and duration of stay to figure out the variety of clothes you'll need, how frequently you'll be moving, and how much you'll want to travel with (quantity / luggage).
- Think about your work, activities, hobbies, social life, and habits to determine the kinds of clothes, accessories, tech, and gear you'll need.
- Pick your luggage and then do at least one or two "test packs" before you leave so you know what fits and what doesn't.
- Don't worry too much! Most things are sold around the world.

LIFESTYLE

"How do you maintain a healthy lifestyle as a digital nomad?"

ONCE YOU'VE FIGURED out where you'll be (and how to get there) and the basics of how you'll work (and with what technology), it's time to sort out both what lifestyle adjustments you'll need to make to your new / temporary home as well as what balance works for you between vacation mode and normal life.

As with everything, all the factors are intertwined, but your lifestyle choices will significantly impact your budget, work, and the experience you have in each place and throughout your digital nomad experience.

Will you be living like a local as much as possible? Or will you be heavily engaged with the local expat community? Or will your habits tend to overlap more with vacationers or backpackers?

There's no right answer, and it can always vary and adjust as your priorities shift or perhaps depending on location or time of year. Sometimes we want to invest heavily in special experiences, socializing, or networking - whether that costs us time or money or both. Other times, it's more important to hunker down, work, and save money.

There's also always a consideration of how involved you want to be with the local lifestyle and integrating into the country's culture versus staying in an expat bubble. (More on this from a philosophical perspective in the *Local Culture* chapter.)

Picking Priorities

What you focus on will depend on the factors you've decided will make you feel successful as a digital nomad. Those priorities may be the amount of income you're able to make each month, or the number of countries you visit in a year. Or perhaps it is having certain kinds of local experiences or going on adventurous side trips.

When it comes to socializing and how you spend your free time, will you want to be more immersed in a new culture and spend months developing a new life in that city or country? If meeting people and relationships are important to you, is it focused more on social or professional networking?

While we all have apps, devices, activities, commitments, and people demanding our attention constantly, it can be even worse for digital nomads. Now, on top of the existing distractions and commitments, we've added countless new inputs and stimuli and opportunities.

FOMO (fear of missing out) grows even stronger when you feel that you're missing new places to explore, new foods to eat, new people to meet, new things to try - every minute of the day.

Plus, instead of having the security of your routine and lifestyle creating a boundary around your time and what's feasible, you now can theoretically pursue re-creating all those instagrammed moments scrolling through your feed.

So what do you do? How will you manage the 24 hours you have each day to you prioritize the aspects of your life that you need and want to ensure you are successful, happy, and healthy?

One post by another digital nomad explores how having a strong understanding of your purpose is critical to succeeding in the adventure of living and working on the road, though it probably applies to any situation:

> *Amidst my quest for life changes and pursuit to hike the AT, I read a book called* Appalachian Trials: The Psychological and Emotional Guide to Successfully Thru-Hiking The Appalachian Trail *by Zack Davis. This is an amazing book*

full of not only tips and techniques for successful long distance hiking and a book full of life lessons…

Most people, when preparing for such a trip, hyper focus on the physical things because they are the things that need to be figured out before you start. Gear, food, money, survival skills and other temporary issues are the primary focus while many neglect preparing themselves mentally and emotionally.

"When it comes to backpacking 2,220 miles, the greatest determining factor of success is purpose." – Zack Davis

To our peers, we have done the most exciting thing ever. We packed up our lives, defying our friends, family and employers to set off on an adventure that most people can barely comprehend, let alone do themselves.

While our world is moving at a blistering pace as we experience new people, places and cultures, everyone else that was important to us is continuing to pursue their passions in life without us.

Minimally we share each other's lives bidirectionally through the lenses of social media, photos, videos & blog posts but that is no substitute for active in-person participation with each other.

What is the purpose of sacrificing relationships, careers or doing any of this without knowing our why?

BEN SCHMIDTKE

We've adapted Ben's adaption of *Knowing Your Why* for digital nomads:

- I am becoming a Digital Nomad (or whatever term you prefer) because… *(this is your why)*
- When I successfully *(define a milestone)*, I will… *(these are the personal benefits you'll acquire upon reaching that milestone)*
- If I give up on that milestone I will… *(these are the negative repercussions of failing to achieve that milestone or embody your vision of success)*

The goal with the "Knowing Your Why" exercise isn't to induce panic or set such high stakes for yourself that you inevitably fail and spiral into a depression. Goodness knows that's not what we're going for – quite the opposite.

But it is important to know why you're making this choice and what your vision of success looks like - and what you're risking for it.

Awareness is a gift, and understanding your goals and motivation is a critical step in making progress towards achieving them.

Self-Care is Critical

It's fun to travel and live in new cities and countries. It's thrilling and gratifying to take side trips and see incredible sights and places. It's exciting to have a community of people around you, always ready to go out for a meal or drink. It's (superficially) rewarding to have an instagram feed chock full of enviable photos.

But realistically, you will still have to take care of the normal aspects of daily life – work, eating, sleep, chores, relationships, personal needs. You'll also be adding challenges due to constant change and upheaval, taking away most of your comforts and known variables, and manage all that for an extended period of time.

We mentioned in the introduction that for most people, this is a shift from a stable lifestyle and routine into frequently changing circumstances and standards of living. It's important to evaluate what you do in your daily routine that you need to incorporate wherever you are in order to stay healthy and happy.

While the freedom of choosing where you go, what you do, when you do it, and having a flexible lifestyle is the draw of becoming a digital nomad, it is also a challenge to often have less control and typically sacrifice the simplicity of a routine.

There are many routes to developing a sustainable lifestyle that suits you, and it will likely take practice over months and testing out several locations before you figure out your priorities and personal needs. It can be an incredible journey of self-discovery through which you'll gain insights into your strengths, weaknesses, and preferences.

What do you need to be happy and healthy? When and where and how are you most successful?

The answers to these questions can range across many factors - learning which times of day you are most productive for work, when you like to play and socialize, what activities you find exhausting and which are restorative, what foods comfort you and when you can be an adventurous eater, when you feel lonely and what connections you need to feel supported, and so on.

Whether it's adjusting to time zones, local foods, cultural differences, working conditions, homesickness, loneliness, stress, finances, or any other number of challenges, there will be many moments that are physically and emotionally exhausting.

Listen to your body and monitor your emotions. Do you need to have alone time and a certain amount of sleep each night to reset? Do you need to schedule calls with friends and family to feel connected to people that are important to you? Do you need to balance food tourism and social drinking with healthy eating and working out?

"Macro-recovery" is a real thing: our bodies and minds need time and care to stay in a healthy place or bounce back from rough moments.

Whether it's readjusting after a long travel day or staying healthy with a night-working schedule or restoring ourselves with alone time, sometimes it's not reasonable to expect ourselves to snap back immediately.

Our Western culture has a mindset that one night's sleep, a few pills, or a healthy juice is going to solve any problem, and we're shocked when we stay tired, get sick, or struggle with emotions.

A great night's sleep and a healthy meal can make a huge positive difference, but more often than not, it's about more prolonged self-care and attention than the quick-fix we crave.

Living on the road and working on your own terms, you're even more responsible for figuring this out for than in your previous routine. It's critical to recognize what you need and make sure you get it.

Katherine says:

I'm still perfecting my process and learning my needs, but a few things that help me are: staying in touch with my therapist via Talkspace, practicing yoga - even if it's only a few minutes, eating healthy food and minimizing my alcohol consumption, sleeping 6-8 hours a night, maintaining a daily writing routine, and spending some time alone.

Ideally, I also have some positive social interactions with people I genuinely like and enjoy. I really appreciate time with close friends and family who give good hugs and cuddle puddle for movies.

I rarely can fit it all in every day, especially when also working and / or doing activities, but I try to do what I can.

The more you observe your routines and daily experiences and compare that with your moods and health, the easier it is to recognize patterns.

We encourage you to constantly assess your priorities, keep your "why" in mind, and remember to be patient and practice self-care.

Again, being a digital nomad is not a long-term vacation – it's a lifestyle. So, just like in "real life", you'll be learning and improving how you live and work and travel over the long run.

The chapter on *Social & Relationships* talks more about how to navigate some of those interactions and establish a support system to help you.

Food & Drink

One of the biggest parts of daily life (and a personal favorite to which we devote a **lot** of time and attention to) is food and drink. Obviously, that is easily an even more exciting experience that can run the gamut between street food gambles to top restaurant tourism.

Whether you decide to eat local and cheap or try the finest dining available in each location (or a healthy mix of both and the spectrum between), how you approach eating and drinking will have significant impacts on your budget, health, and time.

Beyond thinking about how you want to eat your way around the world, there are considerations about what's possible and available in each destination on your itinerary.

First and foremost: Water.

In much of the Americas and Europe, it's fine to drink the water, though you might have to adjust to the taste. However, in more rural areas and most of the developing world, you'll need to buy bottled water or drink filtered water. Some people use filter water bottles, which is another option.

But water isn't only a consideration for what we drink. In some cases, it might not be safe to brush your teeth with the water or get it in your mouth while showering. Sometimes you can adjust to this over time, and every person is different in terms of what their body can manage.

Water also comes into play when thinking about what you eat - are raw fruits and vegetables a viable option given the local water? In some countries, the water both grown in the produce and that it's washed with might not be safe (or, more often, comfortable) to consume. It might be necessary to eat only cooked vegetables in some countries, or at least start with cooked and ease into raw as you spend more time adjusting your body.

Pro Tip:

A lot of travelers use Lifestraw or a UV travel tool to have a sustainable and safe water solution. Usually establishments that cater to tourists serve filtered water, so it's good to check that (and you may have to ask for water in many restaurants). Otherwise, 1L water bottles typically cost around $1 in those developing countries where tap water isn't safe to drink.

In many countries, you may find that you just unavoidably have stomach issues – perhaps it's uncomfortable enough to make you want to leave, but maybe it's a manageable downside given other aspects of living there.

Katherine says:

When I spent 6 weeks in India doing a yoga teacher training with my mom, we both had upset stomachs and diarrhea pretty much the whole time.

We drank a lot of ginger lemon honey in hot water, drank bottled water only, and tried to listen to our bodies about what we could manage eating each meal, and so we were able to travel and practice yoga without any significant interruptions. We also kept pepto-bismuth and anti-diarrhea pills readily available.

Was it uncomfortable and not always pleasant? Obviously, yes, but it wasn't enough to really disrupt what we were doing or cause us to alter our itinerary. It became a joke for us that now is part of our bonding experience and some of our funny tales from our travels together.

Other food and drink considerations include what meat may or may not be available given local geography and/or religion, which also applies to alcohol. Availability can range from strictly illegal and nonexistent to limited to foreigners only to more of a lax suggestion. Do your research beforehand to avoid any legal issues and to understand what's socially appropriate.

Lastly, don't forget to have fun and explore as much of the local specialties and delicacies in each place!

Whether it's getting a taste of an ingredient in its native environment or trying something truly bizarre, culinary explorations are an exciting part of travel and one of the key ways to learn about the culture and connect with other people - locals and travelers alike.

Fitness

Staying healthy on the road is a challenge, but it's an important one to take on. Fitness is not only about looking good and staying healthy, but it's a critical component of keeping up your lifestyle as a digital nomad. Exploring is always easier when you're feeling good and capable of doing the activities at hand.

Whether they advertise it or not, many gyms will negotiate a month-long deal (or whatever time-frame makes sense for your travels). Yoga studios are increasingly common around the world, and running is typically available either on treadmills, outside on streets or in parks, or even perhaps with a local running group.

> Katherine says:
>
> *A handful of people on Remote Year usually tried to negotiate a monthly option for a group to sign up at a nearby gym, typically between $15-50 per month.*
>
> *I recently ran my first ever half-marathon, in our 11th month of Remote Year (December) in Cambodia. Running outside is a great way to stay in shape, experience the local culture, and really earn your experience with the local climate (because everyone talks about the weather, even abroad).*
>
> *I also practice (and occasionally teach) yoga. When I practice, I like to do classes, so I listen to Amazing Yoga classes on Vimeo or use Yoga Studio, which is great for beginners.*

Cities often have community organized or sponsored activities in public places, from yoga to bootcamps, which can be a great way to combine fitness with exploring the city and meeting people – as is finding workout groups on social networking apps like MeetUp.

Entertainment + Activities

Entertaining yourself and having fun is an area that overlaps more with the typical tourist activities offered and also can often parallel your interests back home. Your interests and hobbies may still be available in your temporary homes as a digital nomad, from going to performances to trying local beers to spending your weekends exploring the outdoors.

We won't dive in too deep here with specific suggestions since there are so many resources available between guide books and other digital nomad forums as well as local listings found on Google and Facebook, and no one source is appropriate for every form of entertainment at each price point and interest.

In cities, there are often performances happening any day of the week – musical concerts, theatre, live music at bars, and traditional cultural events – so it's definitely worth looking up major venues and their calendar of events. If your schedule is flexible with work, it's great to buy cheaper matinee performances or see things at different times or days. The experiences can range from world-class to quirky local, and either way is a great way to have a unique cultural experience when traveling or living abroad.

Music festivals are their own form of tourism, so if you enjoy live music or big events with thousands of people, those can be a great way to either have a special once-in-a-lifetime experience or help guide your travels if you plan around various festivals.

Katherine says:

I've seen some strange but endearing and interesting shows over the years as a traveler, including this small sampling:

A black-light show in Prague about Alice "after the looking glass" that included unexpected sexual explorations

A water puppet show with traditional Vietnamese music in Hanoi

A classic Italian opera in Buenos Aires that played up the BDSM undertones at the third biggest opera house in the world

Don Giovanni performed in the Estates Theatre where Mozart originally debuted the opera

A terrifying "interactive" performance by a rogue Nepalese man in a concrete block classroom in northern India

Book of Mormon and then Ralph Fiennes in Shakespeare's Richard III in London

I've discovered them from reading guide books, seeing street posters, being handed leaflets, googling venues, and word of mouth. I typically pay anywhere from $5-40 USD for a ticket, and I try to budget for at least one per month.

It's worth considering how much you're willing to branch out from your interests and whether you will approach entertainment as a form of tourism and learning, not just a way to keep your attention occupied outside of working hours.

There are religious holidays and festivals, temples and churches and synagogues, traditional dance and music performances, and many other local events happening that could be completely open to the public, available with a little digging, may require a local contact to bring you, or are (sadly) potentially off-limits. But they're often the most incredible memories we have of a place and people, so being open, curious, and jumping at the opportunity to take part or witness can tremendously change your experience at the time and in retrospect.

Weekends and side trips (if you have a home base to travel from) are a great way to see more of the country and culture than what the city or your locale has to offer. These can be arranged solo with a bit of research and a leap of faith or through tour companies, and many locals have lots of advice and opinions about where to go, how to get there, and what to do.

41

Outdoor and adventure activities are another incredible side of travel and exploration. While cities offer one aspect of the culture, the natural landscape of a country not only provides fun activities, but also insights into how the country and culture developed the way it did. What are the natural resources and how did the environment create the structure, traditions, and labor of the country? How has it shaped the history and present - and how will the current state of affairs impact the country's future?

But outside (pun-intended) of the cultural appreciation of exploring the countryside, there are many fun and exciting activities to do: rafting, kayaking, surfing, canyoning, hiking, skiing, and more, and each place has unique features of the physical and human landscape that make the experiences all the more memorable. Get out and explore!

Key Takeaways: Lifestyle

- Becoming a digital nomad is (usually) a huge lifestyle shift. Be conscious of why you are making the change and what you need in your life.
- Know when to say YES and say NO – invite unexpected encounters but for the sake of budget + sanity + available time, learn to say no as well
- Pay attention to your Micro + Macro-recovery needs.
- When it comes to planning out your schedule, consider: balancing work and activities, local schedule (when are things open, holidays closing, religious impact), and how much time you need to devote to planning / organizing your DN life (booking travel + new accommodations, researching, planning activities, etc). Do you need to establish routines?

- Remember: there is no one right answer, and your lifestyle can always vary and adjust as your priorities shift or may change depending on your location, workload, or the time of year.

LOCAL CULTURE

"Why do we travel? What is the point of going abroad?"

[Note: Given the global political climate, the scope of the book, and the level of quality and detail we're aiming for throughout the chapters, this one is a bit more serious and philosophical.]

THESE ARE BIG QUESTIONS, and hard to answer. In fact, they're impossible to answer in a way that will ring true for everyone. Of course, there are standard answers that work superficially: people talk about how traveling really "changed their lives" or helped them "grow as a person."

Great! Life-changing is often good, and growth *definitely* has positive connotations. But it's hard to say what all that actually means. Can we hold ourselves and each other to a higher standard of self-awareness and honesty?

It's hard to establish a rubric for the impact of traveling and living abroad. We can track our progress at work by changing roles and titles, salary increases, the teams of people that we manage. But can you quantify the value of experience?

Go deeper: How has traveling *truly* changed the way you live your daily life – especially in a way that is positively impactful for others? What is the mark and measure of that personal growth?

Traveling Through the Looking Glass

Culture is often that elusive and illustrious aspect that makes travel different from everyday life. In our native context and society, our own culture is rendered invisible by exposure.

But when we set foot into another place, we often find ourselves transported like dear old Alice, and it seems as though everything in the world around us is fascinatingly strange.

When we travel, the contrasts stand out and capture our attention. And when we return home, we see our home in a new light, even if only briefly before it fades into familiarity again. Humans are drawn to difference: our eyes pause and ears perk when something is amiss.

The customs and traditions, arts, foods, laws, religions, morals, and knowledge of a people comprise the rich tapestry that is any culture. The threads are the same— nature, beliefs, food, drink, love, sex, community—but how they're woven together varies, and we are, at the least, curious about unfamiliar embroideries.

Travel is intoxicating and exhilarating. Our senses are on high alert: every detail is unknown. Minor interactions and exchanges require our full attention, and our standard rate of success and failure has flown the coop in the face of the unfamiliar.

It is a series of endless gauntlets being thrown down at our feet, and we seek out greater challenges. Go to a new place: mission accepted. Interact in a foreign language: yes, please. Navigate uncharted territories: game on. Set off alone: bon voyage.

The daily grind of a "normal life" at home easily becomes a Sisyphean task not worth the effort when the same stone will always roll back down the same hill. But surmounting challenges in new locations makes us feel powerful and defiant. *Let me push a different rock up a new mountain, just to prove I can.*

Gauntlet: Leave it all behind. Work while you wander. Buck convention. Succeed where others fail.

Meeting "The Locals"

The world doesn't need any more Christopher Columbuses to lay claim to new lands, and the people and cultures we encounter do not exist merely for our own delighted "discovery."

Once we've taken the bait, left home behind, and set off on our journey, what - and who - are we expecting to find?

IMAGES AS ICONS

Katherine says: *Stick with me on this one! ;)*

When I studied Art History in college (started as a math major, but I got hooked on how my professors used art to show us the world in a new way), we spent some time on the "Orientalist" works of 19th century Western European artists.

In particular, we looked at French paintings of northern Africa and the Middle East. The words that come to mind at first glance are "luxurious", "decadent", and "exotic". There's a richness to the paint itself, a warmth and vibrancy of color and texture, and subject matter that - especially for its time - was well outside the mainstream.

But that was exactly how and why it worked, why Delacroix, Ingres, and Gerôme found fame in their day and ours: depicting a world of sensual decadence, images exempt from their culture's rules by virtue of being a representation of a foreign land.

Thanks largely to these scintillating scenes, Western culture then and now imagines other lands as occupied by erotic reclining nudes in tiled baths, young women peering at us below shaded brows, snakes writhing along shoulders, turbaned men outside desert fortresses, corpses splayed on rich fabrics in orgiastic rapture.

Is it all wrong and entirely inaccurate? No.

You'll find ornate tiles and nude baths in Morocco. Sheiks rule the Emirates and wear long white robes with headscarves. Snakes charmers still hypnotize reptiles and humans in city squares.

It is the fiction rooted in truth that makes it compelling.

Our professors cautioned us against accepting the role of unconscious voyeurs. These artists, and their patrons, wield tremendous power of suggestion. Their invisible brushstrokes, lifelike flesh, and precise architectural perspective persuade us: Relish the richness of my representation; be seduced by a world so unlike your own.

But images are not historical documents, and Orientalist paintings are not an anthropological study. (We won't even get into the problematic terminology.)

These depictions do not bear witness or tell authentic truths. Worse, they often preclude a platform for people to tell their own stories, show their own selves, or paint their own world.

The allure of an image is undeniable, and we will seek experiences and environments based on our Instagram feed's saturated scenes. While these are enticing, don't let them be defining.

Challenge the representation you've been shown, and seek alternate portrayals, not only for the sake of satisfying your desire for a unique experience but to bear witness where it is needed, to learn from the direct source, and to facilitate growth in a truly meaningful way.

IT'S HARD NOT to stereotype and compartmentalize. Our brains need to do it to simplify the world around us.

But when we travel and seek out new environments, new people, new cultures, it's important to allow the overload to happen on occasion. To stop ourselves from categorizing everything so we're open to recognize unexpected patterns and outliers.

When we arrive to a new place, how do we want to observe and engage the local culture? How will we treat the people we interact with? It's easy to fall into the habit of "us" and "them," but we all lose when we hold the world around us at arm's length and treat people as flat characters in the narrative of our lives.

Alondo, a fellow Remote Year participant, wrote a blog post about his experience traveling with the program and the group, drawing a parallel with Westworld, a tv series that is "set at the intersection of the near future and the reimagined past, it explores a world in which every human appetite, no matter how noble or depraved, can be indulged."

I wasn't engaging the places at a meaningful level. I was simply visiting. Ticking off checkboxes and collecting passport stamps. So what if I spent a day volunteering at a school or a community garden? Had I really done anything to change their lives for the better? Was I, at least, not making it worse?

In story of my life, I've always been the hero, idealistic with the best of intentions.

But that wasn't the truth. We know where that leads. I'd been seduced by the pleasures of the park. Saying yes became an escalating endeavor of taking chances. What was off limits? Where would I draw the line?

I began behaving as if there were no consequences. Eventually, I said yes to everything: side-trips, hookups, drugs. Everything was new, and my options (and budget) seemed endless. This pleasure cruise was a once in a lifetime experience.

I found myself caught up in the fantasy, not worrying about the consequences of my actions as none of it was "real." The outside world lagged behind at a glacial pace, and what I did here would have no lasting impact.

48

We don't travel with conscious bad intentions. We set off on our journeys to grow, to change our lives for the better. Our quest is knowledge, experience, and depth.

But evolution and wisdom aren't bestowed upon us with a passport stamp at a certain country or after achieving a milestone number of days on the road. It is a slow and conscious process. It is adapting to new environments and constantly seeking awareness. It is, in part, approaching the people and places with curiosity and respect.

It is acknowledging that we are just as much characters passing through other stories as anyone is an extra in ours, and it is considering what part we want to play. "Street vendor 14" may briefly star in our Bolivian street meat adventure anecdote, just as he may occasionally tell the tale of "tourist 57,963."

Whether the interaction is fleeting or lasting, our behavior and attitude impacts the people around us. We're not only witnessing and recording our personal experiences, we're written into other narratives.

Consider how you want to represent your country, religion, culture, age group, and any other category you (or others) might associate you with. Every moment is an opportunity to give others an insight into your world as well.

Combating Cultural Colonization

So *how* do we learn about and engage with the local culture in a productive and meaningful way?

There's a wealth of resources available at our fingertips with the internet, so even if your begin with simply reading the Wikipedia entry, you can start getting insightful information about the place and its history, and use that high-level knowledge to guide more specific searches.

Guidebooks are typically focused on informing a tourist with limited time in a place, and as such they can be a helpful tool as a digital nomad for initial information and activity planning, but may not go into the depth or complexities that are truly insightful to the culture.

Search for novels and nonfiction books to read more about personal narratives and historical experiences of a country or people. Look up local calendars see what holidays, events, lectures, concerts, and other activities will be happening while you're there.

Podcasts can be another helpful way to learn. There are good travel-centric podcasts like Rick Steves, Amateur Traveler, and The Budget Minded Traveler. You can also search podcasts (on the iTunes store, for example) to find episodes that feature information or another perspective about a specific location, sight/site, religion, artwork, or cultural tradition.

> Katherine says:
>
> *When I was traveling around SE Asia on my own, I downloaded any podcasts I could find related to Hanoi, Luang Prabang, Siem Reap, etc. I got some good tips for foods to eat and activities to do, and it helped me anticipate some of the cultural experiences I would have. It also confirmed whether I'd enjoy certain places and informed my itinerary because I could compare my views and style of travel with the narrators'.*

Then there's the approach of meeting locals, making friends, and having more personal and firsthand experiences.

If you're a digital nomad, consider working from a coworking space at least a few days a week or at the beginning of your time somewhere so you can attend their networking or happy hour events. That can also be a great way to ask for introductions to people with specific knowledge or hobbies.

Once you've made a local friend (or more!), you can (hopefully) ask deeper questions, engage in challenging but respectful conversations, share perspectives of each other's cultures, learn more about their culture and home, and perhaps even experience things like a family dinner or a special occasion or celebration.

Institutions and Grassroots Learning Organizations

It is inspiring to see what people have created and improved upon throughout history - consider the limits that past generations made do with given the technology of their time (not to mention war, healthcare, education, etc).

We may be iterating much faster now and experiencing exponential improvements over shorter time frames, but we're standing on their shoulders and are indebted to countless available resources all facilitating that growth. Whether it's creative inspiration or cultural appreciation, understanding and appreciating the past is not only informative but often also inspiring.

So where can we go to be informed and inspired? The opportunities available in different places typically depend on the scale and development, but most cities will have cultural institutions like galleries and museums (art, history, ethnology, textiles, music) and performance venues (theatres, music halls, festivals).

Walking tours are a common way for people to get to know a new city, whether it's as part of a short visit or as a way to orient yourself in your new home. Standard daily walking tours often free (don't forget you're expected to tip $2-5 at the end), and the guide will meet in a designated location once or twice a day to lead a tour for whoever shows up.

Paid tours can ensure your guide has more expertise or the tour centers around a niche focus, like a colonial architecture tour in Cambodia, a night tour of castles in Prague, or a local street food tour.

To find those institutions and tours, local guidebooks and online blogs are great resources. Simple googling the city and "museum" or "show" can lead you to the civic institutional pages or venue calendars. As you do your research, you may also learn about other particular local activities like cooking classes or graffiti tours.

Volunteering, if you can find a productive and positive program, can be a great way to meet people, learn about the community, and contribute. But be careful about volun-tourism and whether your participation will yield a positive impact over the long-term. One-time interactions with children and animals are often not as helpful as they feel.

Sadly, there are also sometimes issues with for-profit schemes taking advantage of tourists trying to do good deeds, like many orphanages in SE Asia, so it's worth doing your due diligence on these before giving your time or money.

Tourist Resources

TripAdvisor is a popular app because it has tons of web traffic and recent reviews, and they also offer top things to do in a city. They also feature offline guides that you can download in advance to have a map, restaurants, and things to do available any time.

MeetUp allows people to find and connect around certain hobbies or activities, so you join a group and attend events in the local community.

Instagram can actually be a good way to find out about things to do and places to go. You can follow accounts that enjoy similar activities as you do or are traveling through a particular region, search hashtags to see what people are doing in certain cities, or look up cafes / restaurants / hotels and see what images people are sharing.

Backstreet Academy has activities in 40 cities in Asia, so you find a location, choose an activity with a local, and book it. The options range from fishing, cooking, weaving, to bike trips, forest walks, sailing, and bird watching. https://www.backstreetacademy.com/

Katherine says:

I used Backstreet to book a weaving class in Luang Prabang, Laos, and a stone carving class in Siem Reap, Cambodia.

For the weaving class, they sent a local high school student to accompany me and translate since the young woman teaching me weaving didn't know English. It really helped me appreciate both what I saw for sale in the markets (those $8 scarves take a day of labor) and how a woman my age lived and worked in another country.

In Cambodia, the artisan taught me and another woman how to carve a small sandstone tile. Not only was it a great present for my dad, but it gave me a better sense of the scope of what I was seeing at the Angkor Wat Archaeological park. Seeing the work and skill required to make one simple tile makes those ornately carved temples even more impressive and hints at the people and labor that went into them.

VAWAA - Vacation With An Artist - is a website created and run by an alum from the original class of Remote Year. An artist and designer, she looked for ways to "immerse herself into the local culture, make things with her hands, and get inspired by learning something new." She noted that there were others like her expecting the same from their travels, but there was no easy way to find local artists and designers in cities they would visit. Thus the idea of 'Vacation With An Artist' was born. Through VAWAA, people can find artists in cities around the world and book a 4-10 day vacation with them to learn a new skill. https://vawaa.com/

Google! Get in there and search for the things you're interested in + the destination city or country you're going to. Whether that's theatre, kitesurfing, local brewpubs, meditation retreats, coding meetups, or anything else, Google is your friend.

(Refer back to the *Lifestyle* chapter for other resources and ideas for activities.)

Immersing Appropriately

When it comes to traveling to another place, it's important to remember that *we* are the visitor in someone else's home. That means finding a middle ground of being true to yourself and also respecting, and abiding by, local traditions, customs, and laws.

While religion can be a significant source of division, it is also a rich aspect of culture. Consider ways in which you can learn about and experience the local religious beliefs and traditions, perhaps not only to gain insight into their culture but your own. The primary world religions (Christianity, Islam, Hinduism, and Buddhism) have been evolving and interacting for centuries, and there's considerable overlap as well as interesting differences between them.

Though we all enjoy our personal luxuries and preferences, not all of it is possible when in another setting. Sometimes living elsewhere means adapting to a different lifestyle for a period of time, but that's usually part of what leads us to that tremendous growth and change we referenced earlier in this chapter. See how the absence of alcohol or the alteration of clothing style changes how you approach the world and experience it in turn.

The adjustments of being abroad may entail:

- Understanding when certain foods or beverages (like pork or alcohol) aren't available in every establishment, store, or perhaps even the entire country
- Dressing appropriately for both specific sites (like temples) and general respect for the local culture (even if you see tourists in muscle tanks and booty shorts in more conservative countries, it's still probably not best to wear those kinds of outfits/articles of clothing)
- Knowing local laws and how they apply to foreigners (from chewing gum in Singapore to women driving in Saudi Arabia)
- Researching local hand gestures, typical manners, and physical interaction protocol (how to wave / point at people and things, how close people get, how they greet each other, what's acceptable between genders)

For solo female travelers, minorities, and members of the LGBTQ community, there may unfortunately be additional risks or concerns in going to certain places. Often, most are safe to travel to with appropriate research, planning, and precautions.

But regardless of what is right or ideal, we must negotiate with reality. That may mean changing certain behaviors or methods of travel, and you may interpret it anywhere from being a standard inconvenience of travel to an imposition on your identity.

Each individual will perceive and define threats and untenable circumstances differently, so all we can advise is to identify your requirements of safety and acceptance, and plan where you go and what you do accordingly.

The famous travel guide himself, Rick Steves, gave an interview in 2009 where he addressed his documentary about Iran, the international consequences of Obama's victory, and some views on Americans and tourists. A few of the questions and his responses:

What's the most important thing people can learn from traveling?

A broader perspective. They can see themselves as part of a family of humankind. It's just quite an adjustment to find out that the people who sit on toilets on this planet are the odd ones. Most people squat. You're raised thinking this is the civilized way to go to the bathroom. But it's not. It's the Western way to go to the bathroom. But it's not more civilized than somebody who squats. A man in Afghanistan once told me that a third of this planet eats with spoons and forks, and a third of the planet eats with chopsticks, and a third eats with their fingers. And they're all just as civilized as one another.

Do you think Americans are more provincial or racist than people in other countries?

The "ugly American" thing is associated with how big your country is. There are not just ugly Americans, there are ugly Germans, ugly Japanese, ugly Russians. Big countries tend to be ethnocentric. Americans say the British drive on the "wrong" side of the road. No, they just drive on the other side of the road. That's indicative of somebody who's ethnocentric. But it doesn't stop with Americans. Certain people, if they don't have the opportunity to travel, always think they're the norm.

Echoing Paul Bowles' famous line, what's the difference between a tourist and a traveler?

I'll give you an example. A few years ago, my family was excited to go to Mazatlán. You get a little strap around your wrist and can have as many margaritas as you want. They only let you see good-looking local people, who give you a massage. There's nothing wrong with that. But I don't consider it travel. I consider it hedonism. And I have no problem with hedonism. But don't call it travel. Travel should bring us together.

That same week, I was invited to go to El Salvador and remember the 25th anniversary of the assassination of Archbishop Oscar Romero. I thought, "I'm not going to be any fun on the beach in Mazatlán, I have to go to San Salvador." So I went down there and I had a miserable, sweaty dorm bed, covered with bug bites. We ate rice and beans one day, and beans and rice the next day. But it was the richest educational experience. It just carbonated my understanding of globalization and the developing world, and Latin America. I was in hog heaven. And I've been enjoying souvenirs from that ever since.

[The Other Side of Rick Steves]

Key Takeaways: Local Culture

- Consider yourself, the people and cultures you'll be interacting with, and the larger world as you define how you want to travel and what your goals are. Dig deeper to clarify what that means in the big picture as well as how it translates to your daily life as a digital nomad.
- Research cultural institutions and tourist activities as well as other ways of engaging with locals to have meaningful learning experiences and interactions.
- Learn what's acceptable, traditional, and legal where you're going to ensure you're abiding by the law and respecting local customs.

SOCIAL & RELATIONSHIPS

"How do I make friends as a digital nomad? Does it get lonely?"

ULTIMATELY, your success as a digital nomad (and, perhaps, elsewhere in life) will come down to your ability to experience and sit with discomfort. Because being a digital nomad is still real life. It's challenging and uncomfortable. You will have some terrible, no good, very bad days.

Take all the normal elements of daily life – work, eating, sleep, chores, relationships, personal needs – and then magnify any challenges due to constant change and upheaval, taking away all your comforts and known quantities, and do all that for an extended period of time.

That's the reality of being a digital nomad, and if you enter the experience fully cognizant of that, you can help set yourself up with the support networks and social life that will help you be happy and productive.

The lifestyle can be a strange mix of more alone time (and loneliness) than we would have at home, paired with intense bonding experiences with the people we do encounter and spend time with.

Socializing on the Road

Parties are typically easy to find – people don't tend to need help with this. If you just head to the bars and clubs, you'll meet travelers, backpackers, other expats, and locals all out for a good time.

Going to cafes and restaurants is another way to meet other travelers as well as make local friends. You may meet other digital nomads at work in cafes, or you might see billboards with flyers for shows and events. Be friendly to local business owners and ask for their advice about how to find things you're interested in or that are particular to the area.

Another good way to make connections is to reach out to alumni from your college or university who are in that city. Whether you are looking to grow your network, get local advice, potentially connect for professional purposes, or have an easier start to a friendship, the common bond of the shared experience often makes people willing to meet up and help out a stranger.

For more professional interactions, go to events at coworking spaces, Meetups, LinkedIn activities. We discuss more resources for meeting people in the *Lifestyle* and *Local Culture* chapters.

Tinder and dating apps are popular tools on the road as well, used for both dating (or hook-up) opportunities and casual social interactions. Make it clear what you're doing and looking for in your profile (how long you'll be in town, what you enjoy doing), and start a conversation around what you're interested in - ask about their favorite restaurant, ask them to meet up, ask what they think of something you've seen already, etc.

Staying Supported

Having a network of people that understand the realities and can support you is critical to your success (and sanity). Whether that's your family and friends back home or new relationships you've created while on the road, identify who you can lean on (as well as who you will commit to supporting in return). Try to establish a routine of keeping in touch, whether by messaging, emails, or regular calls.

One of the benefits of traveling with a program (we outlined some of the current options in *Housing*) is that you are with a group of people experiencing the same things at the same times. You'll all understand, for example, the shared experiences of stomach bugs in

Bolivia, being in London for Brexit, and celebrating Christmas in Cambodia together.

Within the framework of any program or group, there is a high risk of being in an insulated bubble, and it inevitably impacts your experience and engagement locally. But it can be a good short or long-term solution for having a social network physically present for chapters of your digital nomad lifestyle.

Whether you choose to participate in one at the outset of your experience or integrate it later on, it's worth considering programs to help you grow connections to like-minded people who will have more shared experiences with you.

Then there are ways to find or create formal support systems. Set up calls with a therapist at home if you have one, or Talkspace and Better Help allow you to communicate with a personally assigned therapist via their respective apps and platforms.

Katherine says:

As of this writing, I've been speaking with my same Talkspace therapist for almost two years. I send short (or very long) messages through my browser or app, and she responds within 24-48 hours.

Once I began communicating with her, I found myself starting to better understand the boundaries I wanted and needed to have in my other relationships. I also know that I will always get a timely, thoughtful response and that our conversations are intended to be primarily one-sided.

We hire accountants for our taxes, lawyers for our businesses, and doctors for our bodies - why not have professional guidance for the situations in life that we aren't sure how to process or approach?

Keeping Ties Back Home

Social media is one of the primary ways we all keep in touch with friends and family near and far, and it's no different for digital nomads.

Documenting your journey on Instagram, Snapchat, Facebook, a blog, Medium, LinkedIn, or other forum is a common way to provide a window into your experience for others (as well as a helpful record and reflection tool for yourself later!).

Make sure the people in your life know what platforms you will be using, and if they aren't familiar with it, set up time to teach them how to follow along.

From time to time, it's worth cross-posting so that people can find accounts they may have overlooked early on. While it might seem self-promotional to share, it's more often appreciated than not. The people who care about you want to keep up with what you're doing.

Whatsapp is the most common messaging tool for international travelers. Not only does it allow for easy contact over both data and wifi networks, it has many other useful features. You can create group chats and send images, videos, location pins, contacts, which can be great for practical purposes as well as feeling close from far away.

Katherine says:

I have a "Big Family Text" group with my mom, stepdad, sister, and dad, and other chat groups of different familial relationship permutations. My family knows way more about my life from various Whatsapp chats than any other source.

With my Remote Year family, we have a main chat group for our whole community, a "Les Partay" group that originally started for coordinating at Lollapalooza Argentina but has lasted 11+ months, a "Ladies Night" group, and groups for particular side trips, events, and housing assignments.

Pro Tip:

The best approach is to download and start using the app while in your home country with your original SIM card so that your account is tied to that number.

Then, as you travel and swap out SIMs, Whatsapp will ask if you want to update the number – answer no ("Keep" your original number). This makes it easy for people to find and keep in touch with you.

Think about the relationships you have with your friends and family, and consider how you can transition that into your lifestyle on the road.

Do you need to call your mom once a week? Will you talk via a Whatsapp voice call, Skype video, or a Google Hangout?

Do you have a tradition with a friend that you can schedule and do virtually even while you're away? If you have a happy hour at work, can someone dial you in to participate from abroad?

One of the biggest benefits of having a local SIM card and data is that you can easily make a call (typically using Whatsapp, Skype, a Google Fi number vs regular cell minutes).

If you know the time zone differences and the schedule of your friends and family, you can make a quick call while running errands or relaxing at home. Quick chats can help maintain the relationship and make it feel more "normal."

Key Takeaways: Social and Relationships

- This lifestyle can be lonely and challenging, so consider how to establish or maintain the relationships and support network you need.
- Pick a platform to share your journey on, and make sure people know how to follow along!
- Use Whatsapp for chats and voice calls with contacts on the road and friends & family from home.
- Make new friends and find social activities by going to cafes, reaching out to alumni, trying social apps, and being friendly ☺

WHAT NOW?

HOORAY!

You've finished the book. We hope it was every bit as useful and informative as you hoped (and, honestly, more!).

If you haven't yet begun your research and planning, we advise you to go through the *Self-Assessment* and then tackle financial + location scouting first. From there, everything tends to fall into rotation as the lifestyle is a changing and evolving one.

You'll now find several bonus sections – interviews with digital nomads, the *Digital Nomad Tool Kit* (where we've compiled the self-assessment, budget, packing list, and all our recommendation + resource links together), data from our digital nomad census, and an *About Us* section

Check out our website for updates, and don't hesitate to get in touch with us with questions and feedback. Our individual contact information is in our *About Us* profiles, and we can both be reached via:

DigitalNomadHelp.com/Contact

If you have enjoyed this book, please let us know. If there is something you think we should improve on for the second edition, let us know that, too.

Lastly, we *really* appreciate if you would take a few minutes to leave a review with your honest opinion of *The Digital Nomad Survival Guide* on Amazon.

Good luck – we know you can create the life of your dreams!

APPENDIX

DIGITAL NOMAD CENSUS RESULTS

What is a Digital Nomad?

DURING OUR RESEARCH for *The Digital Nomad Survival Guide*, we sought out digital nomad communities for interviews, frequently asked questions, and crowd-sourced advice and travel tips in order to ensure the book has the most up-to-date and relevant information we can give you.

We also conducted a survey to help quantify the demographics, spending habits, and locations of digital nomads. The survey respondents are an extremely diverse group of people: 31 different nationalities, new and experienced nomads alike, across a wide range of professions. The results help paint a picture of who constitutes a digital nomad.

First, let's briefly talk about the term "digital nomad." It's not the only term for what we do, but is the current popular term for someone working remotely while traveling or living away from home. It quickly and accurately describes our digital and nomadic lifestyle: our work relies on technology and internet access, and we are traveling to place to place without a permanent home.

The Digital Nomad Census Survey

We wanted to help define digital nomads: who they are, how they travel, and what they spend. These are our results based on the communities we reached out to. We may reopen the survey for a second edition to get more data and improve the accuracy of our results.

On a demographic level, we learned that a digital nomad is…

- **Evenly split on gender**: Men and women were split close to 50/50, with a small skew toward more female nomads.
- **Millennial**: Most respondents were in the 25-34 range, although approximately 20% of those surveyed were in the 35-44 year old bracket.
- **Newly nomadic**: About ⅓ of the respondents said they had been living the nomadic lifestyle for 6 months or less. Of those, ⅔ of those were in the millennial 25-34 age range. (63% of those who said they had been location independent for 3+ years were 44+ years old.)
- **Educated**: 70% of respondents had a bachelor's degree or higher.
- **Decently wealthy**: 50% of respondents had a monthly income of $2,000 or more.

The demographic part of the survey was in-line with our expectations. For the most part, being a digital nomad is a newer lifestyle trend, adopted by educated people with steady income streams. It is someone who is setting out for adventure but plans to go home to their home country at some point (60% had some future plans to return home).

What does a digital nomad do for work? We found that digital nomads were professionally ...

- **Their own boss**: 63% of respondents identified as a freelancer, working on their own startup, or some other form of self-employed income. No respondents identified as being unemployed.
- **Working a wide variety of jobs**: There were many different job titles represented amongst the respondents, the largest group was software engineers – at 22% – followed by writing, consulting, and eCommerce at

around 9% each. After that, it was hard to group - people ranged from fitness coach to interior designer to accountant. Not included in our survey, marketing is also a common nomad career field.

What we learned was that despite the stereotype that only programmers work remotely, there are increasingly more positions and industries that can be done away from the office. And ultimately, it's easier to do when you report to yourself. Perhaps this will change over the years, as we already see about 20% of nomads replying that they work remotely for an organization that was mostly non-remote.

What best describes their travel plans?

- **Go anywhere!** When asked where they currently were working, 43 countries were represented. The largest groups were Thailand, Colombia, and Indonesia respectively.
- **Slow-to-medium travel pace**: Almost half of the respondents said they travel to a new location once every few months.

Thailand had the largest number of respondents, but many countries and destinations were represented in the survey.

We asked several more questions relating to each individual's monthly expenditures, which you can find in our finances chapter.

If these results don't necessarily reflect who you are as a person, it's important to note that the takeaway here is that anyone can be a digital nomad - each passing year, technological improvements mean the constraints of an office become less and less of an issue.

PART ONE
INTERVIEWS WITH DIGITAL NOMADS

In the following section, you will find interviews we conducted with a few digital nomads.

In most cases, they were new, just like you, within the last year. You might be able to gather some insights into what they do, their plans for the future, and their advice for those who are just starting out.

LAUREN HOM, ILLUSTRATOR

LAUREN IS a designer and illustrator who specializes in lettering. She creates temporary and long-term artwork on chalkboards, walls, and digital for clients that range from small businesses to huge corporations. She recently launched an online course, Passion to Paid, to help teach people her process of making a creative side project into paid work.

Peter, Katherine, and Lauren all met in Montevideo on February 1, 2016 as members of Remote Year's second group. As we worked on writing and planning the book, we decided it would be an amazing opportunity to collaborate with Lauren on the cover.

We also wanted to share some of her story and tips about living and working as a digital nomad, and she graciously agreed to answer some questions about her lifestyle.

How long have you been a digital nomad, and what prompted you to start?

I've been a DN for 1 year now, but I was working remotely before for 2 years. One morning I woke up and thought to myself, "I've been living in NYC for almost 7 years and now that I work from home… I guess I can work anywhere...so why am I still here?" And then I just went.

How often do you currently travel?

I've been moving every 3-4 weeks for a year. I'm going to slow it down to every 3-4 months hopefully, or permanent base and do mini-trips every few months.

Where do you reside currently and why?

I'm still nomadic so no real residence, but I'm in Hoi An, Vietnam right now having a little R&R to celebrate a month of hard work.

Where were you born? Where are you currently living and why?

Rancho Palos Verdes, California. I was living in NYC before because of the career opportunities and creative scene. Currently living... nowhere really.

What is the most important possession you own?

My laptop. My sketchbook comes in at a close second.

What is your best memory traveling?

Can't think of one specific moment...but my favorites have been those moments during late-night conversations with new friends that I realized that we'd be closer friends. Just those little moments of deeper connection and understanding that make you feel really warm inside.

What's been the most difficult challenge of being a digital nomad, and how have you overcome it?

One thing I wish I had known before working remotely while traveling is that you can't have it all. I've been able to visit so many amazing places, but it's definitely not a vacation. But it's also not "just a regular day at the office." When work is busy, it's easy to feel like you're missing out and not exploring and enjoying the new city you're in (like you would if you were just visiting). But if you treat it like a vacation too much, then you feel like you're not working hard enough (at least I do). It's a really hard balance to strike, but I've just had to adopt the mentality that when I'm working, I'm working and when I'm playing, I'm playing. Keeping it separate has been the most effective for me.

NUSEIR YASSIN, VIDEOGRAPHER

NAS MIGHT NOT CALL himself a digital nomad per se, but he's been living the lifestyle since 2016. His primary work involves running his Facebook page, Nas Daily, where he creates and posts a 1-minute video every day while traveling to new countries and exploring the culture there. He's created videos ranging from highlighting the differences between North and South Korea to the delicious meat-loving meals in Serbia.

Subscribe to his channel for motivation to travel or expand your bucket-list. http://www.nasdaily.com

Nas is a great example of a digital nomad who picked up his old life and went out to pursue his dreams. Growing an engaged audience from 0 to almost 100,000 subscribers is no easy feat. We were lucky enough to sit down with him and pick his brain.

How long have you been a digital nomad? What inspired it?

I've been a "digital nomad" for like 233 days as of this writing. I had this idea in my mind for far too long, and at some point I thought I should act on it. The thought was that: why does it make sense to spend the best eight hours of your day, five times a week holed up in an office? If you didn't care enough about your job, that seemed a bit transactional; I give you the best time of my day and of my life, and you give me money that I can spend on the weekend getting drunk. It seemed like a vicious circle that ended up nowhere, and frankly was quite boring considering we all knew what the end outcome was. So this is why I was inspired to just pack my bags and go do videos around the world!

What has been your favorite memory?

Ah, I wish I had a favorite memory. I guess when I went to Easter Island. I titled one of the videos "best day of my life." And it was. The idea that I was on an island in the middle of the ocean making videos and getting paid to do so, only 180 days after quitting my job, made me feel really good.

Where do you call home currently?

Home for me is very hard to define, but I think home is where I feel like I don't have to take videos of things. As of now, home stands in New York City. That's where I can relax and not do videos.

I noticed you taking videos in NYC as well - how has that helped shape your definition of home?

I think whenever I feel comfortable in a place, I do terrible videos. The sense of urgency makes great videos because you know you only have 1 shot at making this video. Just one. And you need to keep going to keep your life interesting.

So, it turns out, for me home is where I feel comfortable, where I don't feel like I need to make videos. I went to Israel, my original birthplace, to see if I felt comfortable. I didn't!

Nas Daily videos, in some way, have helped shape my view of the world. It helped me as much as it helped the viewer.

What's been the most difficult challenge of being a digital nomad and how have you overcome it?

The first five days of going into any country are always the hardest. I don't know what videos I want to make and I don't know how the local audience is going to respond to my arrival. Some countries are very welcoming, others just don't care. The only way to overcome being lonely in a new country is to make videos that resonate with locals - that's how you get to make local friends.

Could you give an example of a country or experience that resulting in the locals not responding well to your arrival, and then about a country that was super pumped about your being there?

I think Germany is one of those countries. I arrived there to visit my brother for his graduation, and I made a couple of videos about some German landmarks. I launched them, boosted the post in

Germany to try to get to locals, and nothing. Nothing happened! Usually when I arrive at a new country, locals reach out and tell me about more interesting things to do, but not in Germany. I think there are three main factors why this happened:

- People don't speak English well, so they are less interested in English content and more in German one.
- Facebook is not heavily used in Germany, and I only publish my content on Facebook.
- My content wasn't very touristy because, well, I wasn't a tourist there. I was there on a family mission!

In terms of countries that responded well to my content, there are many. Costa Rica is my favorite one though. The minute I arrived, people reached out immediately showing me their pride of their country and their willingness to show me around. Heck, I even had Nas Daily followers in Costa Rica before I arrived there, so it seemed like an extension of the US!

I think the reasons my content did well in Costa Rica is the opposite of why my German content didn't do well:

- People speak English enough to get by.
- Facebook is big in CR.
- I created content from the point of view of a tourist coming to their country, which most Costa Ricans feel is overlooked or overshadowed by larger world events. So the fact that a filmmaker came to their country made them appreciate it more.

Do you have any digital nomad pro-tips?

A very straightforward one: travel light. I gave up all my wardrobe and made four teeshirts that say "Life - 32%" in them with a loading bar to remind me that I need to spend every day as a digital nomad in the best way possible. Makes for good, purposeful travel.

What is the most important possession you own that helps enable your lifestyle?

I travel with a LOT of hardware sadly. I have like 7 chargers.

I made sure to get the top of the line Macbook because this is a career investment. Furthermore, I make sure to use a camera that's not too big but still takes great shots: Canon T6s.

I make sure to get an extra battery for every piece of hardware that I can: my camera, drone, GoPro, etc. I wish I could get an extra laptop battery, but that's beside the point :)

Drones are interesting. They provide a perspective that I've never seen before in my life, and I make sure to include them in my videos as much as possible. It makes it all much better. I carry the DJI Phantom 4 but I'm eyeing the Mavic very badly, just waiting on it to be available!

DOUG MILL, DEVELOPER

DOUG MILL IS a cofounder of a coding bootcamp in Medellin, Colombia focused on helping digital nomads become better coders. "Destination: Dev is a program that brings together 10 like-minded individuals for eight intense weeks of software development education and cultural immersion." http://www.destinationdev.com/

How long have you been a digital nomad? What made you start, and what do you do?

I've been a digital nomad since early 2016. After college, I spent a few years working in a Neuroscience lab at UCSF gearing myself up for a career in medicine or science. While I really enjoyed the content of the work we did in the lab, the hierarchy, bureaucracy, and day-in day-out monotonous drudgery of work in a lab led me to look for a path that would provide me with more freedom. I began learning about software development and teaching myself how to code in 2012 in order to have more freedom in my lifestyle and in the projects I get to work on.

I then attended a coding bootcamp to accelerate my learning, and after spending a few years working for a tech company in San Francisco, the pace of my learning began to decrease and I became increasingly bored with the 9-5 grind. I knew that it was time to move on, so I applied to and was accepted into a Start-Up incubator in Santiago, Chile with a friend of mine to work on an entirely open publishing platform for scientific research.

As that project ran its course, my friend and I got a better idea of what problems we are really passionate about and uniquely suited to solve. I found that the freedom that software development provided me to create a lifestyle that I love has truly changed my life, and now I'm launching a coding bootcamp for digital nomads in Medellín, Colombia called Destination: Dev. Our mission is to provide our students with the skills necessary to work on things they're passionate about in an environment that makes them happy, and our first class is kicking off in June 2017.

What has been your favorite location to live and work as a nomad? What made that place special or advantageous?

By far my favorite location so far is Medellín, Colombia (hence, why we chose to launch Destination: Dev here). Medellín has perfect weather year round, and a beautifully lush, verdant landscape. The city is safe, inexpensive, relatively close to the US, and best of all is still somewhat under-the-radar.

I've also found the people here to be some of the friendliest and most welcoming I've encountered, and it also helps that I've been in South America working on my Spanish here and in Chile for most of 2016. Being able to communicate with the locals makes me feel like less of an outsider and allows me to have experiences I wouldn't be able to if I couldn't speak the language.

Can you give us details about the coding boot camp you're putting together in Colombia? What are your goals for the program?

Destination: Dev's mission is to train current and aspiring digital nomads in both software development and cultural immersion. We believe that immersing our students in a foreign culture and simultaneously pushing them out of their comfort zones socially and intellectually will enhance the learning process. We are also confident that extracting our students from their normal environments will both give them the opportunity to really focus on what they're learning and build a strong community. My two co-founders, Andrew and William, and I have all had our lives changed by technology and travel, and we want to share this with our students.

Specifically, the program is an 8-week course in Medellín, Colombia in which students will learn the basics of programming and web development with technologies like Ruby on Rails, JavaScript, HTML and CSS. During the last week of the course, students will create their own web application from the ground-up. Our students live together in a hacker house in the best area of Medellín (included in the cost of the program), and we provide a number of excursions in and around the city, as well as opportunities for activities and cultural exchange.

We are confident that our students will leave Destination: Dev empowered to create a lifestyle for themselves that they can be passionate about. Whether this means becoming a digital nomad, launching a start-up, landing a high-paying software development job in the US, or using their new skills to boost their effectiveness in a career outside of programming. Our students will be able to write software and explore new cultures with the confidence that they can succeed. And, most importantly, they will know that they have the power to learn anything so long as they are willing to persevere and question   their   assumptions.

PART TWO
DIGITAL NOMAD TOOLKIT

SELF-ASSESSMENT

Note: This is the same as what was shown at the start of the book, if you have already completed this, move on to the next section.

OUR ADVICE on how to approach this self-assessment:

1. Read the questions first.
2. Start a note (on scratch paper or a note on your computer), and answer without editing yourself—think stream-of-consciousness responses.
3. Review your answers and note patterns and inconsistencies.
4. Create a document on your computer and write down your responses, editing if needed to get clear and definitive answers or hierarchies.

We will address these points throughout the book - this is meant to be an initial assessment to get your planning started and creative juices flowing.

Digital Nomad

1. How did you first hear about the digital nomad lifestyle?
2. What appeals to you? Why are you excited about it?
3. What aspects do you think will be difficult for you?
4. What does it mean to be a digital nomad to you?
5. What does it mean to do it successfully?
6. Who do you know that is already a digital nomad? Whose lifestyle is an example for you?
7. Why do you want to be a digital nomad? [aim for a direct, specific, and simple statement]

Circumstances

1. Where do you currently live? [location and residence type]
2. Who are the important people in your life? [family, partner, friends, employer, clients, etc]
3. How will you becoming a digital nomad impact them?
4. Do you have pets, a home, a car, and other major considerations that need to be resolved before you can leave?

Work

1. What is your current job and employment status?
2. Is it already remote / is it possible to do it remotely?
3. Have you discussed it with your employer / clients yet?
4. What technology do you need for work? [hardware and software]
5. How many hours a week do you need to work?
6. Do you need to work in a specific time zone?
7. What work challenges do you anticipate as part of becoming a digital nomad / working remotely?
8. What opportunities will become available as a digital nomad / working remotely? [professionally and personally]
9. What are your favorite parts of your job / work? What are you best at doing?

Travel

1. How long are you planning to be a digital nomad? [up to 6 months, 1-2 years, 2+ years, etc]
2. Why that time frame?

3. Do you have anywhere you need to be on certain dates?
4. How many places do you want to go / how frequently do you want to move?
5. Where are you most excited to visit and live? Why?
6. Will you be traveling alone, with someone else, or joining a group?
7. What country's citizenship / passport will you use for your travels?

Money

1. What do you currently spend on housing each month? Each day? [divide monthly by 30]
2. What do you currently spend on food each month? Each day?
3. What do you currently spend on social + entertainment each month? Each day? [movies, shows, games, happy hours, nights out, etc]
4. What will your estimated monthly income be as a digital nomad?
5. How much will you want to spend on activities each month? [side trips, adventures, classes, big dollar experiences, etc]

Possessions

1. What are a few of your favorite things?
2. What clothes and belongings do you absolutely need?
3. Do you have any medical prescriptions, devices, or other belongings that you need to travel with?
4. What material items in your current life can you live without?

5. What do you want to do with your clothes, furniture, and belongings that you won't bring with you?

Personal

1. What are your daily routines?
2. What do you need in your home environment to be comfortable and relaxed?
3. What do you need in your work environment to be successful and productive?
4. What do you need in your personal life and relationships to feel supported and happy?
5. Do you need significant time alone or do you prefer to be with others?

Congratulations on taking the first concrete step! Thinking through these questions and seeing your answers should already give you insights to what you need and want in your new lifestyle as a digital   nomad.

SAMPLE BUDGET

KATHERINE'S REMOTE YEAR involved 12 months spent in 12 cities + countries, so these expenses reflect the average across South America, Europe, and SE Asia over a year:

1. Montevideo, Uruguay
2. Buenos Aires, Argentina
3. La Paz, Bolivia
4. Cusco, Peru
5. London, England
6. Prague, Czech Republic
7. Belgrade, Serbia
8. Split, Croatia
9. Kuala Lumpur, Malaysia
10. Koh Phangan, Thailand
11. Phnom Penh, Cambodia
12. Ho Chi Minh City, Vietnam

Below is a summary of Katherine's **actual** average expenses (in USD) on Remote Year. This does **not** include any personal, insurance, medical, taxes, gifts, donations, or home expenses (like storage).

Katherine's Average RY Expenses

- Remote Year (Accommodation, Monthly Travel, Workspace, Events, Staff Support): $2000 / month, $27,000 total for the year
- Additional Travel: $200-500 / month
- Food: $400-600 / month
- Activities: $100-300 / month
- Social: $50-150 / month

- Transportation: $50-100 / month
- Work: $100-150 / month
- **Total: $2900 - 4000 / month**

Building Your Budget

When it comes to building out your own budget, use your analysis of your current daily, monthly, and long-term spending to create a breakdown of your expense categories and values. Then use your research of your destinations and their expenses as well as your frequency of travel, major transportation expenses, big budget activities, etc. to create an estimate.

With all that data, you can either start with a daily budget and multiply it out over the course of time you'll be planning for (daily x 7 days x TBD weeks x TBD months), or you can make a monthly, annual, or other long-term budget totals and divide that out to get your daily spending (total / (TBD months x TBD weeks x 7 days)).

Katherine's Budget Building Strategy

When I do my budgets and financial tracking, I create a spreadsheet with an Estimate tab, a Total tab, and then individual expense tabs (cash, credit card, bank, PayPal / Venmo).

On the Estimate tab, I set it up so that some values can be a total (ex: $600 for the year on Activities) and others can be daily (ex: $20 / day on food), and then it will calculate all my average daily, monthly, and total estimates.

I label every expense transaction with one of my Estimate categories, and I set up formulas so my expenses feed into the Total tab for calculations to show me how my actual spending compares vs. estimated expenses across each category for total time, monthly, and daily.

To do it yourself, start by listing out each category of expenses (travel, housing, food, social, activities, insurance, etc), decide on a time-frame for your estimates (total, monthly, daily) and label the next column with that, then fill in the values next to each category with your estimate.

Add a "sum" formula at the bottom, and you've got the start of your budget. Change the numbers to see how it affects your bottom line and get a sense of where you can splurge and where you need to stay tight.

However, Mint and other tools do very similar things with an easier interface if spreadsheets aren't your thing (though I'd say it's well worth attempting and learning how to use spreadsheets! My self-taught skills have gotten me a couple jobs).

PACKING LIST

HERE'S a simplified packing list to help you think through what you may need and want with you, based on Katherine's Remote Year packing and the other nomad packing lists we referenced.

Clothes

- *1+ regular pants (jeans and/or something nice for restaurants and events)*
- *1+ workout / technical pants or shorts*
- *2+ casual dresses and/or nice clothes*
- *4+ regular tops*
- *2+ workout / technical tops*

Jackets + Layers

- *1 long layer (merino wool, hoodie, etc)*
- *1 casual jacket (leather, jean, etc)*
- *1 lightweight warm technical jacket (if traveling to colder climates / hiking)*
- *1 rain jacket / windbreaker*

Accessories

- *1+ bathing suit*
- *8+ underwear*
- *6+ socks*
- *Hats, headbands, scarves, etc – depending on your personal preference, style, and destinations*

Shoes

- *Running shoes*
- *Sandals or flats*

- *Flip flops*

Stuff

- *Toiletries – shampoo, soap, toothpaste, toothbrush, hairbrush, razor, etc*
- *Personal favorite items (slippers, robe, yoga mat, etc)*
- *Travel towel (microfiber)*
- *First aid kit – either a true kit or just the medicines, bandaids, ointments, etc that you think you'll need; headlamp, whistle*
- *Water bottle – maybe a LifeStraw depending on where you travel (though some people complain of leakage)*
- *Travel comforts: airplane inflatable pillow, pillowcase, ear plugs, sleep mask*
- *Laundry: dissolvable detergent, clothes line, wrinkle + odor spray*
- *Dry sack: for packing and keeping things dry / sand-free at the beach*
- *Security: PacSafe or other travel security gear, locks, laptop chains, etc*

Bags

- *Main luggage bag (hard body suitcase, rolling soft side suitcase, duffle, large backpack, etc)*
- *Side trip bag (backpack or packable duffle)*
- *Carry on (rolling, backpack, or duffle – may be the same as your side trip bag)*
- *Laptop bag / purse – consider what you truly will carry every day and feel comfortable, whether that's a tote bag or a backpack or messenger bag, consider pockets, zippers (HIGHLY recommended for safety)*

- *Potential extra bags: fanny pack, small crossbody purse, clutch, zip wallet*

Technology

- *Laptop*
- *Unlocked smart phone*
- *Camera – some people use a real (non-phone) camera or GoPro (or drone!), but most people find it's not worth carrying around, so consider whether you will really use it before buying or packing it*
- *Work tools – if you use a pen + tablet, extra monitor, microphone, etc, consider whether you will really need and use it*
- *Kindle / iPad / tablet – many people like these for reading, watching videos, etc but it can easily end up being extra weight*
- *Headphones*
- *Other: travel adapter, portable charger, portable speaker, external hard drive*

RECOMMENDATIONS & RESOURCES

HERE'S a list of resources mentioned throughout the book. Descriptions are straight from the source, not our words.

* * *

Organization
Tools to help you to stay organized (personally and professionally).

Google Drive
Drive starts you with 15 GB of free Google online storage, so you can keep photos, stories, designs, drawings, recordings, videos – anything.

Google Calendar
With Google's free online calendar, it's easy to keep track of life's important events all in one place.

Evernote
Big ideas, little details, and everything in between. Anything that matters to you can be captured in a note, ready for when you need it.

Trello
Infinitely flexible. Incredibly easy to use. Great mobile apps. It's free. Trello keeps track of everything, from the big picture to the minute details. Trello's boards, lists, and cards enable you to organize and prioritize your projects in a fun, flexible and rewarding way.

Any Do

Get life under control with the ultimate app for getting things done. Any.do is the easiest life manager around, which means people stick with it twice as long as other to-do apps. Over 15M users agree.

Wunderlist
Wunderlist is the easiest way to get stuff done. Whether you're planning a holiday, sharing a shopping list with a partner or managing multiple work projects, Wunderlist is here to help you tick off all your personal and professional to-dos.

* * *

Apps
Apps for communication, social media, and quick time + money conversions.

Whatsapp
WhatsApp Messenger: More than 1 billion people in over 180 countries use WhatsApp to stay in touch with friends and family, anytime and anywhere.

Instagram
Sign up to see photos and videos from your friends.

Snapchat
Snapchat lets you easily talk with friends, view Live Stories from around the world, and explore news in Discover. Life's more fun when you live in the moment!

Medium
Welcome to Medium, a place to read, write, and interact with the stories that matter most to you.

WordPress
Create a free website or easily build a blog on WordPress.com.
Hundreds of free, customizable, mobile-ready designs and themes.
Free hosting and support.

Tinder
Tinder is how people meet. It's like real life, but better.

Every Time Zone
Never warp your brain with time zone math again.

XE Currency
Calculate live currency and foreign exchange rates with this free
currency converter.

* * *

Financial
Tools and services for your tracking, transfers, spending, and
insurance.

Mint
We bring together everything from balances and bills to your credit
score and more. It's your financial life, in one place that's easy to
understand.

Personal Capital
Take control of your money now with Personal Capital. Manage
assets and investments, get objective advice and strategies.

Charles Schwab Bank High Yield Investor Checking Account®

Pay no ATM fees worldwide with our popular online checking account. There are no monthly service fees, you'll earn interest on your balance, and your account is FDIC-insured.

Revolut
The new fair way to instantly send and spend money globally.

Transferwise
A peer-to-peer money transfer service.

Chase Sapphire Reserve + Chase Sapphire Preferred

IRS Foreign Earned Income

World Nomads Insurance

Clements International Property Insurance

TJ Lee, How to Save for a Year of Travel

* * *

Research
Where to find the information to decide where you want to live.

Numbeo
Numbeo is the world's largest database of user contributed data about cities and countries worldwide. Numbeo provides current and timely information on world living conditions including cost of living, housing indicators, health care, traffic, crime and pollution.

Internet Speeds

Wikipedia typically offers high-level summaries of climate data for cities and countries on their individual Wiki pages. Wikipedia also has a list of countries by internet speeds.

SpeedTest

Ookla Speedtest puts the most sophisticated broadband testing and analysis tools into the hands of anyone interested in finding out just how connected they actually are. This free service from Ookla opens hundreds of testing locations around the world to anyone curious about the performance of their Internet connection. Use our service to view your service's performance history, then share and compare with others near you - or around the globe.

Climatelist

ClimateList helps you visualize when is the best time to travel.

STEP Program

The Smart Traveler Enrollment Program (STEP) is a free service to allow U.S. citizens and nationals traveling abroad to enroll their trip with the nearest U.S. Embassy or Consulate.

Teleport

Tell us what matters to you and we'll recommend great places to live. Teleport Cities finds your best places to be in the world, based on how your personal preferences match 254 cities around the world.

Destigogo

We bring you the best travel destinations that truly fit within your budget. We hand-curated 650+ of world's best travel destinations, examined thousands of flight- and hotel prices and collected tons of additional information.

NomadList
Nomad List finds you the best places in the world to live and work remotely.

Digital Nomads Around the World (Facebook group)
This is a place for digital nomads to share advice and tips related to living the digital nomad lifestyle. Sharing our experiences and knowledge can only be a good thing! :)

Katie McKnoulty, Choosing Your Next Destination

Karsten Aichholz, Thailand Starter Kit

* * *

Nomad Programs & Communities
For when you want to spend time with a group of people and hand off some of your responsibilities.

Remote Year
Remote Year brings together a community of 75 interesting professionals from across the globe to spend a year working, traveling, and exploring 12 cities around the world.

Hacker Paradise
Travel the world. Build cool things. Meet awesome people. We organize trips all over the world for developers, designers, and entrepreneurs who want to travel while working remotely or focusing on personal projects.

Embark Together

Embark brings together a talented community of entrepreneurs and creative professionals who work and travel together. We provide the community, accommodation, work space and transportation, so you can focus on what matters most to you.

Wifi Tribe

Every month, we choose a different city to call home. We are inviting a mix of young, wild and free, location-independent professionals to join us anywhere along the way: entrepreneurs, photographers, developers, writers, designers, marketers, adventure addicts...

We Roam

We are a travel-while-working program that curates trips around the world for select remote workers who want to pursue their love of travel, without putting their careers on hold.

Terminal 3

Terminal 3 is more than a vacation. It's your opportunity to savor local cuisines, connect with locals, make lifelong friends and find yourself in the process. And when you travel with us you make the world a better place by giving back to local communities.

Roam

Roam is a network of global coliving spaces that provide everything you need to feel at home and be productive the moment you arrive. Strong, battle-tested wifi, a coworking space, chef's kitchen and a diverse community.

Nomad Cruise

Join us and over 150 other remote workers, entrepreneurs and digital nomads as we cross the Atlantic on a 15-day cruise. Be part of an experience where connections are made, thought-provoking events are held, and ideas are shaped and created. Become part of a community that will change your life even long after the cruise.

* * *

Housing
Where to look for where to live.

Airbnb
Airbnb is a trusted community marketplace for people to list, discover, and book unique accommodations around the world — online or from a mobile phone or tablet.

Booking
Booking.com B.V. guarantees the best prices for every type of property, from small, family-run bed and breakfasts to executive apartments and five-star luxury suites.

HostelWorld
Hostelworld Group is the leading global hostel-booking platform with Hostelworld, Hostelbookers and Hostels.com in its portfolio operating in 19 different languages. Connecting young travellers with hostels around the world, Hostelworld has over 8 million reviews across 33,000 properties in more than 170 countries.

Couchsurfing
With Couchsurfing, you can stay with locals in every country on earth. Travel like a local, stay in someone's home and experience the world in a way money can't buy. There's a community of Couchsurfers near you. Many cities have weekly language exchanges, dance classes, hikes and dinners. Make new friends.

* * *
Travel
Trains, planes, and automobiles: how to find and book 'em.

FlyOnward
FlyOnward is an exclusive Flight Ticket Rental Service. We provide you with international flight tickets (travel itineraries) with your name on them to use as proof of onward travel plans when you travel abroad.

Rome2Rio
Rome 2 Rio is a comprehensive global trip planner that helps you get from a to b worldwide. You can enter any town, address or landmark as your destination and Rome2rio will instantly display flight, train, bus, ferry and driving options with estimated travel times and fares. Our travel search engine contains route information from over 4,800 transport operators in over 158 countries.

Google Flights
Book plane tickets through Google Flights. If you're not ready to book a trip, you can use Google Flights to track prices for a flight or route.

Skyscanner
Skyscanner compares hundreds of airlines worldwide for free. It finds the cheapest flights fast: saves you time, saves you money.

Kayak
KAYAK searches hundreds of other travel sites at once to find the information you need to make the right decisions on flights, hotels & rental cars.

Expedia

Plan your trip with Expedia. Buy airline tickets, read reviews & reserve a hotel. Find deals on vacations, rental cars & cruises. Great prices guaranteed!

Orbitz

Plan your trip with Orbitz. Buy airline tickets, read reviews & reserve a hotel. Find deals on vacations, rental cars & cruises. Great prices guaranteed!

Travelocity

Book & Save at Travelocity. Best Price Guarantee On Over 325000 Hotels. Flight, Packages, Cars, and Travel Planning. Wander Wisely Today!

AirAsia

AirAsia offers the lowest fares online to over 100 destinations across Asia with numerous frequencies a day. Fly with the World's Best Low-Cost Carrier today.

Priority Pass

Priority Pass is the world's largest independent airport lounge access program.

Lounge Club

LOUNGE CLUB™ membership is a great way to get access to airport lounges throughout the world. We are an independent airport lounge program, which means that you have access to our partner lounges regardless of the airline or class of travel you are flying.

* * *

Working

The tech tools to work-from-wherever.

Slack

Slack brings all your communication together in one place. It's real-time messaging, archiving and search for modern teams.

Basecamp

Trusted by millions, Basecamp is the leading web-based project management and collaboration tool. To-dos, files, messages, schedules, and milestones.

Asana

Asana is the easiest way for teams to track their work—and get results.

Box

Box is changing how you manage content across your business from simple file sharing to building custom apps.

Dropbox

Dropbox simplifies the way you create, share and collaborate. Bring your photos, docs, and videos anywhere and keep your files safe.

Zoom

Zoom unifies cloud video conferencing, simple online meetings, and cross platform group chat into one easy-to-use platform.

WeWork

Find inspiring workspace, connect with a global community, and benefit from 100+ services to help grow your business.

Startup House
We aim to transform ideas and projects in successful companies, providing the support needed at the earlier stage for entrepreneurs. We do this through accommodation, access to office space, incubation and connections to entrepreneurs in the network.

Copass
A global membership that lets you access a network of independent coworking spaces, fablabs, hacker spaces or any type of collaborative spaces and people with one single account.

Workfrom
The best places in a city to work remotely, based on recommendations by actual remote workers. See WiFi speeds, plugs, food and more before you go.

Coworking Map
Our goal is to map all the spaces on the planet, marking its location by anyone!

RemoteSeats
We take beautiful unused restaurant spaces and make them available to a community of business travelers, creatives, and entrepreneurs.

Pomodoro Technique

MeetUp
Find Meetups so you can do more of what matters to you. Or create your own group and meet people near you who share your interests.

Tim Chimoy
Digital Nomads: The dark side of freedom

* * *

Technology
How to keep your stuff safe and stay connected.

iCloud
iCloud makes sure you always have the latest versions of your most important things — documents, photos, notes, contacts, and more — on all your devices.

Dropbox
Bring your photos, docs, and videos anywhere and keep your files safe.

T-Mobile Simple Choice Plan
Each of our Simple Choice Prepaid plans come with unlimited talk and text to keep you connected. All you have to do is choose how much high-speed data you want per month.

Google Project Fi
Welcome to Project Fi, a wireless service from Google. By designing around how people live, we've created a service that feels like it was built for you.

Pre-Paid Sim Wiki
This Wiki collects information about prepaid (or PAYG) mobile phone plans from all over the world. Not just any plans though, they must include good data rates, perfect for smartphone travellers, as well as tablet or mobile modem users.

Apple MacBooks
MacBook, MacBook Air, and MacBook Pro

Microsoft Surface

The tablet that can replace your laptop.

Chromebook

The Chromebook is a new, faster computer. It starts in seconds, and offers thousands of apps. It has built-in virus protection, and backs up your stuff in the cloud.

Jono Lee, Securing Your Digital Life

* * *

Packing

What to bring, or not - that is the question.

Tiago Almeida, Travel Light

TJ Lee, How I Packed For a Year of Travel

Jessie Lang, The Ultimate Guide to Packing for a Year

Arestia Rosenberg, What Do I Pack As A New Digital Nomad

Katherine Conaway, Remote Year Packing List

* * *

Lifestyle

Stay healthy and happy on the road.

Ben Schmidtke, When The Going Gets Tough

Lifestraw

LifeStraw is committed to redefining the safe drinking water space through technology innovation and product quality and design.

Amazing Yoga classes on Vimeo
Amazing Yoga teachers power yoga in Pittsburgh PA and conducts retreats, teacher training, and workshops worldwide. Classes are challenging and inspiring that promote healing, creativity, purpose, and a path to total wellness.

Yoga Studio app
Yoga Studio includes 65 ready-made classes. Choose your level (beginner, intermediate or advanced), duration (15, 30 or 60 minutes) and focus (strength, flexibility, relaxation, balance or combination) to find the perfect class for you.

Yogo mat
Maker of YOGO, a compact folding travel yoga mat. Take Yoga Anywhere!

Manduka mat towel
Explore Manduka's selection of Yoga Performance Towels! Super-absorbent, soft & modern, shop by practice, style & type and find the best Yoga Towel for you!

* * *

Local Culture
Connect with where you are and who's there.

Alondo, WestWorld blog post

Rick Steves Podcast

The podcast version of Rick's radio show brings you a weekly, hour-long audio conversation featuring authors and experts talking with Rick about travel, cultures ...

Amateur Traveler Podcast
Which destinations to travel to next and what to do, see and eat there. Learn from the award winning Amateur Traveler podcast.

The Budget Minded Traveler Podcast
The Budget-Minded Traveler podcast is a trusted source for the inspiration and practical tips that make international travel accessible to everyone.

TripAdvisor
World's Largest Travel Site. 435 million+ unbiased traveler reviews. Search 200+ sites to find the best hotel prices.

MeetUp
Find Meetups so you can do more of what matters to you. Or create your own group and meet people near you who share your interests.

Backstreet Academy

VAWAA | Vacation With An Artist
Through VAWAA, people can find artists in cities around the world and book a 4-10 day vacation with them to learn a new skill.

Kevin Berger, The other side of Rick Steves
He may seem like Mister Rogers. But in a revealing interview, the travel guru shares his daring views on Iran and terrorism, spoiled Americans and the best places to smoke pot in Europe.

* * *

Social & Relationships
Long-distance support systems.

Katherine Conaway, I Love My Online Therapist

Talkspace
Chat with a licensed therapist anytime and anywhere with Talkspace online therapy. Join the over 300000 people who are already feeling better today!

BetterHelp
BetterHelp offers private, affordable online counseling when you need it from licensed, board-accredited therapists. Get help, you deserve to be happy!

* * *

Many helpful resources and more can be found on our website:
DigitalNomadHelp.com

The Digital Nomad Census (you can participate too!):
DigitalNomadHelp.com/Census

ABOUT US

Katherine and Peter met as members of Remote Year's second group (Battuta) in Montevideo, Uruguay, when our program started in February 2016.

With Remote Year, we traveled together to Uruguay, Argentina, Bolivia, Peru, the Czech Republic, Serbia, and Croatia.

After a couple years of working remotely and traveling the world both with Remote Year and independently, Peter decided to write a book to help others get real, practical advice on becoming a digital nomad. And this guide truly reflects our lifestyle - it is the result of collaboration of digital nomads working together, remotely.

Peter started the project while living and working in Bali. He asked Katherine to coauthor it, pitching the idea over a Slack call from Bali to Kuala Lumpur. We collaborated via Slack and Google docs to write the book, meeting for an in-person session on the island of Koh Phangan, Thailand.

Lauren Hom, a letterer and illustrator who was also a member of RY2 Battuta, is the designer of the book cover. Katherine and Peter created a Pinterest board, sent her notes and wireframes, had a group kickoff call, and let her work her magic creating our name treatment and   icons   for   the   cover   design.

CO-AUTHOR: PETER KNUDSON

PETER HAS BEEN WORKING REMOTELY for two years, primarily as a senior product manager in the game industry. His day-to-day involves working as a consultant, helping a number of gaming studios and publishers refine their product's user experience and monetization strategies. He has worked on products by companies including The Pokemon Company, Adult Swim, Al Jazeera, and Facebook.

Before working as a consultant, Peter was a senior product manager at Activision and earlier at Zynga and Wizards of the Coast. The games and brands that have his fingerprints on them include *Magic: The Gathering, Peanuts, Downton Abbey, NFL, NBA, Adult Swim, Al Jazeera,* and *Farmville.* He graduated from Harvard University in 2013 with a degree in Economics.

In 2015, Peter was working as a remote employee for Activision, and while his life was good – living in San Francisco in a nice apartment in the Mission district – he realized that he was potentially wasting an opportunity, so he began to explore travel opportunities.

One day, after a Facebook advertisement popped up for Remote Year, he applied to join the second class of remotes. After some soul-searching and a few short weeks, he was in Montevideo, Uruguay, working out of the Sinergia coworking space, the Mission apartment fading deeper and deeper into the background.

His favorite part about the digital nomad lifestyle is the sense of ownership he has over his life. While the responsibilities of "real life" never go away, he feels that the freedom to choose location, work hours, and priorities keeps him motivated to do his best work.

- **Hometown:** Saint Paul, Minnesota

- **Current Role:** Product Manager Consultant at Adrian Crook and Associates
- **Favorite Digital Nomad Location:** Bali, Indonesia
- **Current Hardware:** Macbook Pro 2012, Samsung Galaxy Tab S2, iPhone 6+

Contact:

- LinkedIn: https://www.linkedin.com/in/peterknudson
- Facebook https://www.facebook.com/plknudson
- Instagram http://instagram.com/Plknudson

CO-AUTHOR: KATHERINE CONAWAY

KATHERINE HAS BEEN a digital nomad for almost 3 years, traveling and working around the world since June 2014. She was a member of Remote Year's second group, traveling with them from February 2016 to January 2017. At publication, she's traveled to 40 countries and counting.

Katherine is a freelance producer, consultant, and writer. She contracts with clients to do consulting, strategy, and writing – working on websites, shoots, events, workshops, courses, and beyond.

For 2.5 years, she was the (remote) Head of Production for Public Persona, a brand strategy + creative studio. One of her current projects is doing research, strategy, and PR for Bluffworks, a men's travel clothing brand.

Katherine grew up in Fort Worth, Texas, and went to Williams College in Massachusetts to study math, but graduated with a degree in Art History. She studied abroad in Siena, Italy, which piqued her interest in finding jobs that would help her live and travel abroad.

After college, Katherine taught math for a year at the Casablanca American School in Morocco and then a year of 8th grade English at the American College of Sofia in Bulgaria. She moved back to the US and worked at a wind energy development firm in Austin before moving to NYC to work in production at HUSH, a design studio in Brooklyn, for two years.

Becoming a "digital nomad" was not, actually, an intentional transition. In May 2014, I left my job in Brooklyn and packed up my apartment to visit friends and family for the summer with a plan to return that fall / winter.

However, at the same time, a creative director I'd previously worked with had started her own design + branding studio and asked me for part-time production help. This stream of income allowed me to keep extending my travel plans 3-8 weeks at a time...

While traveling in Hong Kong, 11 months in as a digital nomad, she learned about Remote Year thanks to a friend forwarding an article. She looked at Remote Year's site and contacted the founder, Greg Caplan, to ask about joining the program.

Although I was already working remotely while traveling, I found the program very appealing in spite of the initial sticker shock of the price. The fees covered RY planning + coordinating travel, housing, and events, and the program provided a community and networking opportunities, which added up to a valuable offering and big time-saver for me.

Katherine writes about Remote Year in a publication on Medium and has a podcast about modern work. Sign up for her mailing list to get updates about her travel, writing, and work.

- **Hometown:** Fort Worth, Texas
- **Favorite Digital Nomad Location:** Prague, Czech Republic
- **Current Hardware:** MacBook Air 2013 (Apple refurbished), iPhone 5 & 6, Wacom Intuous Pen & Touch Tablet, Blue Snowball Microphone

Contact:

- Website: http://katherineconaway.com
- LinkedIn https://www.linkedin.com/in/katherineconaway
- Medium https://medium.com/@katherinerc
- Podcast http://modernworkpodcast.com
- Mailing List http://eepurl.com/bGsk71
- Facebook https://www.facebook.com/katherineconaway/
- Instagram https://www.instagram.com/katherineconaway/

ILLUSTRATOR: LAUREN HOM

LAUREN HOM IS A CALIFORNIA-BORN, formerly Brooklyn-based designer and letterer who's currently traveling the world. Known for her bright color palettes and playful letterforms, Lauren has created work for clients like Starbucks, Google, AT&T, YouTube and TIME Magazine.

Her work has been recognized by Communication Arts, the Art Directors Club, the Type Directors Club, the One Club, and the Webby Awards. Lauren is also the author of the popular blog (and now book) <u>Daily Dishonesty</u>.

She finds that she's happiest when creating; so, when she's not working, you can find her baking yummy things, selling your ex-boyfriend's tears, or lettering for lunch around New York City. Lauren's motto is, and will always be, "Work hard, snack often."

- Tumblr: http://homsweethom.tumblr.com/
- Facebook: https://www.facebook.com/heyhomsweethom/
- Instagram: @HomSweetHom
- Twitter: @HomSweetHom
- Dribbble: https://dribbble.com/laurennicolehom
- Daily Dishonesty: http://dailydishonesty.com/

Made in the USA
Monee, IL
01 February 2020

21137101R00113